23/9

HUSBANDRY

Sex, Love & Dirty Laundry:

Inside the Minds of

Married Men

STEPHEN FRIED

BANTAM BOOKS

HUSBANDRY

A Bantam Book / September 2007

Published by
Bantam Dell
A Division of Random House, Inc.
New York, New York

The essays in this collection have previously appeared in *Ladies' Home Journal.*

Book design by Helene Berinsky

Bantam Books is a registered trademark of Random House, Inc., and the
colophon is a trademark of Random House, Inc.

Library of Congress Cataloging-in-Publication Data

Fried, Stephen, 1958–
Husbandry : sex, love & dirty laundry—inside the minds of married men /
Stephen Fried.
p. cm.
ISBN 978-0-553-80665-6 (hardcover)
1. Husbands. 2. Married people. 3. Man-woman relationships. I. Title.

HQ756.F745 2007
306.872'2—dc22
2007012604

Printed in the United States of America
Published simultaneously in Canada

www.bantamdell.com

10 9 8 7 6 5 4 3 2 1
BVG

To Diane

husbandry (hŭz'bən-drē) *n.*

1. The application of scientific principles to agriculture, especially to animal breeding.

2. The application of somewhat less scientific principles (like asking friends really personal questions, quizzing the wife, revealing stuff that could embarrass yourself and others, and yes, okay, maybe reading a few studies) to musings on being a husband.

Contents

HUSBANDRY

Every Journey Begins
with a Pair of Socks

Let's start with my socks. Not the ones I'm wearing, but the ones I wore yesterday. The ones I took off last night and plopped on the floor in the general vicinity of the laundry basket. Yes, those socks. Those size-thirteen socks that are the biggest source of discord in my twenty-year marriage.

When my wife, Diane, comes across my socks—so close to the basket, yet so far from actually being in it— the incredulity begins to bubble up inside her. And then we have "the discussion," which starts out about socks and ends up being about the evolution of the species. It's the same place the discussion about the dirty dishes in the sink ends up.

Now, this discussion about the evolution of the species is actually quite fascinating—as long as you're not in the middle of it. As it begins, Diane, who has a high-school trophy on her shelf for "Best Negative Debater," poses this query: Are these socks (or dishes) left where they are because I don't remember she's asked me a million times not to leave them there, or because I remember being asked, but I just don't care that it matters to her?

While I'm trying to figure out which response would be better for the future of my marriage (or, as the guys in my regular half-court basketball game put it, "Which answer gets me laid?"), my wife, a novelist who also reads a lot of science books for fun, asks a second question. If I don't remember (which is sounding more and more like the right answer here), is it because I wasn't listening to her all the times she asked, or is there something wrong with me physiologically—an actual problem with the workings of my brain, some bad sectors on my mental hard drive? Then she notes that studies have shown that men's brains deteriorate faster than women's, and at forty-nine, my robust lobes have probably started shrinking to the size of raisins.

By this point in the increasingly one-sided discussion, the correct response is clear.

Okay, put me down for the brain damage.

If only it were that easy to escape the discussion. Usually, I am able to wriggle out of this inquisition because my wife knows that I wouldn't purposely do anything to make her upset. But I suspect she also privately takes comfort in the smaller brain theory, which is another example of the big lies women tell men about size not mattering.

What I would never tell her, of course, is that while I really don't remember that I shouldn't let my socks decorate the floor, I also don't really care. Sure, I care that it matters to her. But to be perfectly frank, I doubt I'm ever going to really care myself or even understand why it matters to her. When it comes to socks or dishes, Diane knows I prefer a good, messy pileup and, after a week (or a month) or so, a really good cleaning. For situations where bacteria and decay aren't involved, well, what's wrong with tidying up once a year?

After all, isn't that where the term "spring cleaning" came from?

I know there are some men who undoubtedly remember to put their socks in the laundry and believe in that same-day dish-doing thing. One of my two brothers is actually quite neat (we refer to him as "the mailman's child"), so it is possible for a man to actually care about such things. But most men I know don't. And won't.

One friend of mine believes that the real issue isn't remembering or caring, but rather the sheer volume of wifely requests. "Well, they go on and on about so many things—I mean, how can you tell which ones really matter anyway?" he asks, exasperated. "I think women need to stop every now and again and say, 'This bit is really important, so you can forget the last four hours of stuff I've been going on about.' "

While I have some experience with what he's describing, I still think the reason I can't just throw away a cereal box with five Cheerios left in it lies in the fuzzy area between remembering and caring. So I decided to dig up some of those studies Diane always throws in my face about men's and women's memories and brains. It turns out that the most current work focuses less on brain capacity and more on the gender differences in wiring, especially for cognition and memory. The research shows that women have better "emotional memories" and better "autobiographical memories" than men.

This would support a theory I like: Men are physiologically programmed not to remember that they are supposed to care about stuff like the final resting place of their socks. (On a more serious note, the researchers speculate that having a better emotional memory is one reason women suffer from depression more than men.)

I found another aspect of this study especially revealing. This particular research was done by showing groups of men and women the same series of images and then asking three weeks later what they remembered about them. Apparently, the women found four specific pictures the most emotionally intense. Dead bodies. Gravestones. Crying people. And a dirty toilet.

The women found a dirty toilet as emotionally intense as a dead body.

So here's my query to Diane: It's bad enough that you're burdened with this horrific association; is it something you really wish on me?

Her answer, of course, is yes.

Hoop Dreams for Husbands: Half-Court at Midlife

 Every Sunday morning at 7:30, I bring my wife a cup of coffee in bed. And every time, I get the same yawning response.

"Play nice with the other boys," Diane says before rolling back over to sleep. "And don't get hurt."

It's not exactly an inspiring pep talk as I depart for the gym. But, in many ways, I share her concern about the half-court basketball game I've been playing in, with the same group of guys, since 1991. In our game, where the average player age is now fifty, winning isn't everything. Being able to walk to the whirlpool unassisted afterward is everything. Being able to play the next game is everything.

I'm at the age when most men experience basketball only in memory and on television—which they watch until it's warm enough outside to play golf. So I'm pleased to be part of a group that plays and sweats together, year-round, supported by ankle and knee braces, prescription goggles, taped fingers, and the power of competitive camaraderie.

I must admit that I'm awed by the amount of intense time this group of guys spends in the alternative universe of our half-court-at-midlife game. Not only do we play three times a week, but we also e-mail promiscuously—making sure we have enough players and cyber-trash-talking about previous contests. But only one player has ever said his wife was bothered by the amount of time his family was losing to the game. And that could be because they have four kids whom she left her law career to raise, and because he also has a lot of travel and dinner commitments for work. (He also has the worst injury record in the game: two torn knee ligaments, both of which required surgery and extensive rehab.)

Another player actually came to the gym one Sunday morning directly from the delivery room after his first child was born. He claimed he got permission from his wife, who had just finished twelve hours of labor.

We are still waiting to hear her version of this conversation.

As for Diane, her reaction is always the same. "Just don't get hurt." And when I do get hurt—so far no surgeries, but a lot of very colorful sprains, cycles of excruciating back pain, and an endless variety of contusions and gouges—she never calls me an idiot (although she may be thinking it). She knows the game sustains me in ways that matter to our marriage.

If anything, Diane would like me to play more often. She wants the extra time alone in the house to write. But she also realizes how much I need to interact with a regular group of guys for reasons other than work or family—to re-create a certain bunk-mentality that I associate with summer camp, a dynamic that's increasingly hard to find as the hair under your bandanna grays (or disappears). There's also the purely physical satisfaction of your body doing something perfectly without you even thinking about it. Each of us has become addicted to the autonomic ballet of his best shot.

As the game has evolved, we've gotten to know one another's playing styles, moods, and physical changes intimately. We play only with the guys we bring (based on the principle that if you're going to have a career-ending injury, it should at least be inflicted by someone you know and like). So we are able to experiment with different matchups—except for the two attorneys we call "the Bruise Brothers," who play with such disregard for their own bodies that we allow them to guard (and hurt) only each other.

While this is far from a sweaty support group, we have developed a kind of brotherhood over all these years of playing three-on-three. We're quick to comment on physical changes (in weight or mental acuity) and we minister to one another's injuries (out of a combination of compassion and selfish need to retain our regular players). We also bear witness to the plot twists of our off-court lives and offer whatever encouragement we can. Several years ago, one of our players lost his executive job. That sent a chill through a group that had come together in their thirties when we were young marrieds, but now were staring down the bazooka barrel of middle age. So after years of playing only on Sunday, we decided to add a second game, and started playing on Wednesday afternoons, too.

We told ourselves we were doing this to help our friend through a rough time but, in truth, we created this afternoon "hooky game" to stave off our own midlife crises. It was a much cheaper and less risky indulgence than a sports car or an affair, and if you work through lunch, disappearing from 2 to 3:30 doesn't seem so bad.

We liked the hooky game so much, we added another one on Friday. And so far, the game has worked as preventive therapy: Only one of our regular players has had a true midlife crisis. We discuss this and other personal stuff only after the game. While we try to keep the on-court banter focused on hoop controversies, our postgame discussions have a tendency to suddenly go deep, on politics or business or the most private of matters. And then we get dressed and go back to our lives.

Not long ago, my basketball buddies and I attempted to do something together besides play. It was the first time that we had all seen each other in street clothes. One of the Bruise Brothers was fighting in a celebrity boxing match on a Saturday night, and we decided to meet for dinner and then go watch somebody whack *him* for a change.

The dinner conversation was pretty subdued. Apparently, we have an easier time being loose with our feelings when physically spent. (So if you have trouble getting your husband to open up, try athletic sex, or maybe just have him run around the block a few times.) When the fight ended after two rounds, I wondered if the group would go out drinking together, or visit the "gentleman's club" nearby. While most of our players are married and pretty settled, we do have some single guys in the group, including our oldest player (in his sixties) and our youngest (in his twenties)—we refer to them as "Sanford and Son"—who I thought might push the others into a night on the town. Instead, at 8:45 on a Saturday night, most of us were ready to call it quits.

After all, we had basketball in the morning.

Dead Fathers Society

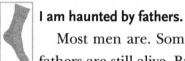**I am haunted by fathers.**

Most men are. Some are haunted while their fathers are still alive. But almost all of us become haunted after our fathers die.

I am reminded of this more often than I care to admit. Holidays, birthdays, every time I take a walk on the beach. Every great sunrise and sunset (he always made you stop whatever you were doing to watch). Often during movies, TV dramas, even those cloying commercials that made Robert De Niro bawl in *Analyze This*.

But, I must say, Father's Day is the worst, and not only for the obvious reasons. It was just after Father's Day that I found out my dad, then only sixty-one, was not going to live much longer. The next time we were all together, a few weeks later at the family shore house, where we pretended everything was going to be okay and went through our rituals of sea-glass hunting, horseshoe pitching, and seafood gluttony, he already knew he was facing the death penalty for not having gotten a colonoscopy.

The last seven months of his life were extraordinarily powerful for me. I will never let go of them, and they will never let go of me. So I think a lot about how the death of a parent affects a guy, both as a man and as a husband.

Men are often very different—to themselves, and to their spouses—after losing their fathers. In some marriages, it might be the first time a wife has ever seen her husband express (or openly struggle with *not* expressing) strong emotion. That's because it's almost impossible to remain stoic once you've been inducted into the Dead Fathers Society.

And it is a society. Anyone whose father is still alive really can't understand. You can sympathize, I hope, but not really understand. And, in some marriages, I'm guessing that's a big problem. Here your husband is finally expressing emotion, and it's not one you recognize or know how to deal with.

My wife, Diane, has weathered my membership in the Dead Fathers Society pretty well. She has never given me the "snap out of it" speech that many spouses deliver—out loud or through their actions—once they realize that grieving lasts so much longer than sympathy. And she has always responded to my need to be comforted, which is one of the most crucial things in any relationship.

Still, I think she is mystified by my need to remind myself of my loss, to purposely make myself upset by it. I'll watch the male version of a chick flick, *A River Runs Through It,* every time it's on—and it's on a lot—because all the fishing and the intergenerational intensity reminds me of my father and brothers. Dad always took us fishing when we were kids, so for his sixtieth birthday we took him to Canada for an amazing fishing trip, which a friend dubbed *A River Runs Jewish.*

Diane doesn't know why I would subject myself to such deliberate heart wrenching. But I know why. If I don't purposely make myself upset about losing my father, the emotion will sneak up on me when I least expect it. This way I can sort of control my out-of-control reactions.

If this makes no sense to you, don't be in a hurry to understand it. Once you're in the society, it'll make way too much sense.

There has been some intriguing research on how losing a parent affects adult children, as individuals and in their marriages. Sociologists at the University of Texas even studied the differences between losing your father or your mother. While both devastate in their own way, the death of a mother was shown to cause more psychological distress, while fathers' deaths drive more people to drink—especially if your father drank. (Married men who lost hard-drinking dads increased their own alcohol consumption by about one hundred drinks a month.) When married people lose their mothers, they report a decline in support from their spouses and an increase in their spouses' negative behaviors (arguing, drinking, having affairs). The death of a father is more associated with a decline in overall "relationship harmony."

So, basically, when we join the Dead Fathers Society—and, statistically, fathers die first—we become more difficult to live with, to ourselves as well as to our spouses. In the Dead Mothers Society, we look to our spouses more for support—maybe to replace what our mothers were giving us—and often don't get what we need.

Either loss can create an incredibly risky marital moment. If you don't figure out how to be there for your spouse during this time of need (based on *their* assessment of need, not yours), you may never be forgiven. But if you do learn how to share "good grief"—which isn't easy because resources are few and expert opinions hard to come by—it can save your life together. I've now watched way too many of our friends go through what Diane and I did ten years ago. Fortunately, the experience has made more couples than it has broken.

As for me, I do my best to survive each Father's Day. And then, the weekend after, Diane and I and our fami-

lies make our annual pilgrimage to the family beach
house. It's a tradition we began as a way of coping with
my father's death, because nowhere is the spirit of Jerry
Fried more present than at the shore. If I'm going to be
haunted, I'd rather be haunted in the sun, with sand between my toes and the sound of squealing children and
seagulls in my ears, searching the shallow surf for those
exquisitely misshapen pieces of sea glass, the junk
turned to jewels that link me to him.

Men Who Diet and the
Women Who Love Them

In most couples, there is at least one lifelong dieter. In our house, it happens to be the husband. When I page through the photo albums from our marriage, they look like an endless compilation of before-and-after and before-again pictures.

When I first met Diane, I was fresh off a professional setback and an ugly romantic breakup, so I was the beneficiary of the only diet you don't need a book for—the "suicidal depression weight-loss plan." I weighed less than I ever had in my adult life. Since then, I probably have lost and gained cumulatively more pounds than you currently weigh. My dieting nickname is "Yo-Yo Moi."

My wife, of course, comes from one of those infuriating families that are naturally trim and well muscled, and when any of them has three pounds to lose, it comes off pretty much effortlessly. I try not to hate them for it. (Although their existence does pose an interesting marital conundrum: Would you rather be married to someone in great shape, or be in great shape yourself? Discuss.)

Diane is upset by my tidal waistline, but not so much because my dating figure was false advertising. (She saw the pictures in my parents' house. She knew what she was in for.) She is upset because of the health risks, and also because I am so predictably miserable when overweight. Luckily, I've never seen any evidence that Diane is less attracted to me when I'm at my largest. This means she either loves me for who I am or is a really great actress (both of which are keys to any successful marriage). But I feel so much less attractive myself when large that her feelings for me aren't my main problem.

Any husband who claims he doesn't care about his weight is just flat-out lying. (If the Tony Sopranos of the world weren't embarrassed about their guts, they wouldn't be wearing oversized, untucked shirts.) I've always known this to be true, but I also thought that the percentage of men willing to admit it would always be fairly small. (Actually, the percentage of men willing to admit anything is fairly small.)

Then came low-carb dieting, which changed the world of weight loss in all kinds of surprising ways. The most significant change to me, a student of the subtleties of husbandry and wifery, is that men now talk openly about dieting—to their wives, and to other guys—in a way they never did before. In fact, they won't shut up about it. Dr. Atkins' greatest achievement might have been to turn dieting into an extreme sport, complete with bragging rights and endless conversations about techniques. Talking about meat and meat by-products has become the new form of male bonding.

I'm still having a little trouble adjusting to this, because my male dieting shame is deeply ingrained. When I was nine, my mom sent me to a juvie weight-watching group for "big-boned" boys, where we got weighed and lectured on the joys of filling up on shakes made from low-fat dried milk and those vile first-generation diet sodas. This group traumatized me for life. In those days boys weren't supposed to think or talk about dieting. Dieting was women's work and involved girly food: cottage cheese, lettuce, diet soda. If boys wanted to lose weight, they were supposed to run faster and jump higher. Women dieted; real men ate real food and then burned it off. And during my dieting career, when I went on earlier fad diets like Scarsdale, I always felt somehow, well, emasculated that I should have to.

My most recent diet began when I realized I had finally outgrown even my fat pants and something had to be done. (You know you're in trouble when you have bigger breasts than your wife.) I bought the Atkins and South Beach books, and before long I wouldn't shut up about carb-counting, either. Neither would Diane, but for another reason. While she is accustomed to being forced to go on whatever diet I'm on, this has usually meant just smaller portions of the food we normally like, or cutting out things that are obviously bad for you. But, in the bizarro low-carb world, most of the healthy food we'd been preparing for each other for the past twenty years (or ordering from takeout) was off-limits.

We suddenly had a marriage without comfort food. Marriages need comfort food.

There are some other low-carb issues that can vex couples. Since the diets actually work better for men than for women, I have heard of couples going on them together and not getting similar results—so the husband suddenly feels more confident and babe-magnetic while the wife is left waiting for ketosis like a late period.

The diet can also change household roles because the only cooking most men know how to do is grilling large hunks of protein, so our few talents are suddenly needed. Although I think most men are like me in that they only want to grill the meat, and still expect their wives to prepare everything else. Grilling allows every man his fifteen minutes of feeling like a surgeon, and then he waits for the "nurse" to mop his brow and clean up.

I think about all this stuff because it keeps me from obsessing over all that fettuccine with broccoli rabe I've been missing. And those soft pretzels—the best ones in the country are made at a bakery just down the street. And the pizza, oh Lord, the pizza. I now have been away from my favorite food group for what seems like an eternity. I get to visit it on very special occasions, but my day-to-day life revolves around Egg Beaters, salads fortified with broccoli slaw, chicken breasts, and carefully counted-out almonds. I dropped just over thirty pounds—and I always love the compliments you get for that, which make it very clear that everyone thought you looked like absolute hell before. But I've never hated eating more.

As for Diane, she has enjoyed the fact that there's less of me and also bemoans the loss of all her favorite carbs. But she knows that, sooner or later, both the carbs and my pounds will be back. I say I'm now in "maintenance" mode, but we all know that's a big lie. In dieting, as in life, you're either on your way down or on your way up.

Potty Training for Husbands

My wife and I have been talking about redoing our master bathroom for almost three years now. We've blamed the delays on disagreements over design, budget, cabinetry, fixtures, and, of course, tile—since you now have to choose not only color but shape, texture, heat-ability, and, I think, aroma. But Diane and I both know what's really holding everything up. We have only enough room for one master bathroom. And while married couples need to be able to share a great many things, I'm no longer convinced that a bathroom is one of them.

It's just not natural.

I believe husbands and wives can work out pretty much anything with time, communication, patience, and perhaps full-contact couples therapy. Anything, that is, except peace in one shared bathroom.

I'm not talking about seat-up versus seat-down stuff. That's never been an issue for us. My wife is a petite little peanut, and the first time I left the seat up she literally fell in. I can't live with that. So I always put the seat back down.

Everything else about husbands and wives and bathrooms, however, is up for heated debate. Take the condition of that seat—its general cleanliness and esprit de corps. All very subjective. A personal preference thing, really. In fact, I foresee a day when the male perspective on this starts gaining more acceptance. Maybe the folks who write those *Everyone Poops* children's books can do a sequel called *Everyone Pees on the Seat.*

Or, take the question (a favorite in our house) of whether the bath mat really needs to be hung up to dry or can be left to dry by itself lying on the floor all day long. I know Diane believes hanging it up is better, based on certain "knowledge" that has been passed down from wife to wife through the generations. But are there double-blind clinical trials that prove one way is better than the other? I'd be happy to volunteer if some husbands' rights group wants to fund such a study.

I don't mean to minimize the importance of the problems caused by wives trying desperately to somehow re-potty-train their husbands. This is serious stuff. One of my basketball buddies admitted to me recently that bathroom battles almost wrecked his marriage. "Our old condo had only one bathroom," he said. "She *hated* me when we lived there. She was always banging on the door and telling me that she *needed that bathroom!*" Finally, they bought a place with enough space to put a dinky water closet for him next to her nice big bathroom. He even agreed to make it the only room in the house he was responsible for cleaning. But she's still on his back about it. He may have to resort to every teenage boy's fantasy—putting his own lock on the bathroom door.

My fantasy bathroom would be a little more elaborate. It would be a room, tiled floor to ceiling, that is completely flushable—push a button and water flows out from up high on every wall and cleans every surface. I would sit in the middle of the room, in a specially made Barcalounger with a hole under the seat, magazine racks all around me, suspended from the ceiling so they won't get wet.

If there were a waterproof TV in there—or even better, a DVD player—I might never come out. Just slide the meals under the door. Use paper plates and plastic utensils, and I'll just flush the whole works when I'm done.

I've given more thought than I care to admit to why there is so much marital friction concerning the bathroom. Much of my thinking has taken place in the cramped, reading-material-free guest powder room, a long flight of steps down from our bedroom, to which I am banished so Diane can be mistress of the master bath. Part of the friction is obviously just competition over access to the nicest bathroom in the house. And there are, of course, the standard battles over the husbandly and wifely understandings of concepts like "clean" or "dry" or "put away" or "mine." I will admit to sometimes walking out of the shower soaking wet to get more soap or shaving cream and then afterward doing only a cursory job of sopping up puddles, *even though I know this is wrong*. And I have been guilty of wiping steam off the mirror with my hand although I realize this could cause smudges, streaks, and other forms of reflective sullying.

But I think there's a bigger issue here. I think wives are, at some basic level, deeply offended by everything their husbands do in the bathroom. Diane daintily refers to her time in the bathroom as "being at my *toilette*," because she doesn't want her endless primping to be confused with what icky boys do in there. Yes, that's right—we actually sit down. On that porcelain thing. And for much longer than *any* bodily process could possibly take. Deal with it.

Now, discussing this issue is one of the last taboos in most marriages. Guys who have seen their wives give birth have still never seen them going to the bathroom. I know in twenty years I never have.

Diane is willing to talk about these issues but only

conceptually, so that I may learn more about the ways of her gender. Apparently women are conditioned from childhood to sit for as few seconds as possible in home bathrooms—and in public restrooms, they are to gymnastically hover without actually touching the seat. I guess this is very traumatizing, so wives can't believe their husbands would ever spend a second longer than necessary actually going to the bathroom.

Just like we can't believe how much time they spend in there *not* going to the bathroom.

Interestingly, I think this is one marital battle of the sexes where husbands might be, if you'll excuse the expression, getting a leg up on the competition. Everything I read about bathroom design suggests more and more reasons to spend extended periods of time there. And everything I read about cell phone, BlackBerry, and wireless laptop use suggests that more and more people are multitasking from the throne. Apparently, nearly forty percent of people answer their cell phones in the bathroom. That number is only going to go up.

As for our bathroom renovation, I'll be curious to see how it finally plays out. Because, regardless of all the debates over glass tile texture, whirlpool depth, and sink-drain feng shui, the only way for us to create a separate little bathroom for me would be if Diane were willing to sacrifice the closet she uses exclusively to store her shoes. I'm afraid that if I ask her to choose between pampering her footwear and having her own bathroom, it could turn out like one of those *Star Trek* episodes where Captain Kirk tricks a powerful robot by giving it two mutually exclusive commands, causing it to self-destruct.

I really don't want to see my wife's brain blow up. Although, if it happened in my fantastically flushable bathroom, I would know how to clean it up.

Love in the
Time of Snoring

When I was a youth and my love life consisted almost entirely of wishful thinking, I dreamed of being "good in bed." With husbandry far in my future, I naively assumed that being good in bed was all about sex. Now that I'm married, I realize it is all about snoring.

It is also all about cuddling, insomnia, and your ability to recognize and appreciate Clean Sheet Day.

Of course, being good in bed can also involve dizzying heights of sexual satisfaction. But I'm not talking about those four to six hours a month (and for most couples, that's a good month). I'm talking about the vast majority of our time in bed, which is spent in an equally intimate activity—sleeping together. Or, *trying* to sleep together.

According to recent research, about twelve percent of married couples in America don't even sleep in the same room. According to my own highly unscientific research—which involves being incredibly nosy with my friends—the percentage of couples who literally don't sleep together is actually much higher. For example, a lot of the couples who leave the TV on in their bedrooms all night long are not really sleeping together. What they are doing is closer to just nodding off sitting next to each other at the movies—something I have, on occasion, been known to do, which is why I have a permanent bruise in the shape of my wife's elbow between my third and fourth ribs. I am proud to say we have never had a TV in our bedroom (or a video camera, a fact which certainly helps me sleep easier).

I think couples who don't sleep together fall into two basic groups. There are the ones who gradually stop sleeping together to "temporarily" accommodate tearful babies who want to sleep with the parents. So the breadwinner starts camping out in the guest room to avoid snoozing during the morning staff meeting (which can impair career advancement), and then has trouble finding the way back to the marital bed.

But mostly, there are the couples driven to opposite sides of the bed—and sometimes the house—by snoring, the sound that makes a grinding garbage disposal seem musical by comparison. The spouses on the receiving end of these snores, often women, used to suffer in snarly silence. Now, however, all the things that drive wives crazy about their husbands are being reinvented as medical conditions—especially snoring, for which there are now some three hundred registered treatments and surgical techniques.

I do realize snoring can be a symptom of sleep apnea, a significant health risk. But I also suspect that a lot of men are being sent off to have an overnight sleep study at a hospital so their wives can get at least one good night's rest.

I went for a sleep study once. I spent Halloween night (the only appointment available for months because so many people are being sleep-studied) attached to dozens of electrodes while Diane was home hogging the covers in peace.

Actually, I should have insisted that Diane do the study with me. Instead of just monitoring for apnea, they could have brought some scientific certainty to the questions that really vex sleeping (or non-sleeping) couples. Such as, who actually snored more often and more loudly, broken down by seconds and decibels. (Since each of us is capable of snoring that could wake the dead, it would be useful to know who was actually more at fault.) Or, who did what to stop the other's snoring. Since Diane is smaller than I am, I can usually just roll her on her side and make it stop, but I have always wondered what manner of nose-pinching, shoving, and other Three Stooges–type techniques she employs to quiet me down. Or, who commandeered which covers for the sleep session. This can be tricky to spot, since from above, it might look like the comforter is over both of us, while Diane could have stolen the entire sheet from underneath. I propose a MattressCam.

Since we generally sleep with four pillows—one for each head, and another two that can be used for sitting up and reading or covering the other ear—we don't have many disputes in that area. But it might be worth experimenting with only two to see who ends up with them by night's end. Sort of like Pillow *Survivor.*

Now, that's my idea of a sleep study.

As for the more clinical study I had, the results were inconclusive. They suggested I lose weight (although isn't the result of almost any test you have over the age of thirty-five that you should lose weight?). And I should stop sleeping on my back. But mostly they reassured Diane that all my huffing and snorting and irregular breathing would not kill me anytime soon. It was just garden-variety, mild apnea—clinical snoring—which afflicts a great many men and quite a few women (and, I think, almost all dogs).

The treatment? Deal with it.

So now it's just one more aspect of our very high level of marital sleep management, which we've been perfecting since we moved in together twenty years ago. Luckily, we started out compatible in many areas. I am naturally right-bedded while Diane is a lefty. (I can't imagine how couples who both need the same side solve this problem. Weekly, daily, or hourly rotation?) We both would rather sleep in a room that is too cold than too hot. And we both like a firm mattress. In fact, Diane could sleep on a slab of granite.

I did feel a little inadequate at first because I am spooning-impaired. But it turned out that Diane can't fall asleep being spooned anyway. In fact, she believes that nobody really can—it's just a movie conceit.

But there are other ways of being attentive in bed. I'm a very light sleeper, and I will invariably wake up if Diane is having a bad dream. I really enjoy being able to soothe her in her sleep. Reciprocating, however, is a little trickier. Like many women at midlife, Diane finds that her slumber is increasingly fragile. So, if I have a bad dream, it's actually risky for me to wake her up to seek comfort. But she still insists that I do it. It's important to be able to ask for, and to accept, that kind of attention from your spouse. It creates a feeling of closeness and security that is the best part of sleeping together.

As couples grow older, however, some sleep issues aren't about the bedroom at all. Like many men, I can fall asleep almost anywhere—on planes and trains, on the couch watching TV (I miss the second half of most DVDs we rent), even at the tail end of family gatherings or parties. Sometimes I even snore sitting up, which is very charming. My young nieces and nephews find this endlessly amusing. I'll sometimes sputter awake to find them giggling and preparing to toss coins into my mouth.

Diane, however, does not find this amusing at all. So my next couples sleep challenge is not only being good in bed, but being good in chair.

Present Tensions

I run into a friend of mine shopping at a jewelry and crafts store. He has a look of sheer panic in his eyes, and his lips are so tightly pursed that his beard and mustache practically meet. I know that look. It's a very specific form of performance anxiety that starts gripping married men in early December.

It's fear of "gift impotence," and he has an especially bad case. For the past few years, he has been buying his wife pieces of jewelry made by the same offbeat artisan, whose stuff he knows she loves. So the gifts have essentially been preapproved; she might as well have registered for them. But now he has already bought her the earrings, the necklace, the bracelet, the stickpin. Unless his wife starts an extensive program of piercing in the next week, my friend is screwed. He actually has to shop this year. And he'll risk buying something that could fail miserably, causing the entire holiday to unravel.

It suddenly occurs to me why my father was so happy when my mom discovered those shiny little Swarovski crystal animals. He never had to take another gift risk in his life.

The holidays are hell for husbands, in all kinds of ways that wives will never appreciate. And most of us are smart enough not to complain about these pressures (except to one another) because how much sympathy can we really expect? After all, in most families, nearly every aspect of holiday planning, decorating, buying, wrapping, cleaning, and cooking is handled by the women. Husbands contribute so little to this entire enterprise, except, of course, our unsolicited advice to our wives and mothers and sisters that they shouldn't get so stressed out, for which we get the stink eye or slapped upside the head.

When I casually mention to Diane that my friend and I chatted about the pressure to nail that perfect gift, she gives me The Look. "It's the only thing you have to do for the holiday," she says. "And you have the entire year to do it!"

I will admit to feeling a bit guilty that wives do most of what sociologists call "kin keeping." Diane does everything from sending birthday cards to my family members (which she has to "sign" from me) to cata-

loguing the familial intrigues, maintaining mental flow
charts about who's angry at whom and who'll be touchy
about what.

Still, in defense of husbands, we may not get very involved with the planning for the holidays, but once the
family celebration actually starts, we're called upon for
a lot of heavy lifting—physically and psychologically.
The winter holidays are more intense than all the others
put together. I think I've seen more raw human emotion—family members uncontrollably laughing or
weeping (or both at the same time)—during December
than during any other month.

Every holiday season, we receive the same plain white
postcard from one of Diane's old friends. Always un-
signed, it reads simply, sarcastically, "It's the most wonderful time of the year."

Tell me about it.

For us, it's doubly wonderful. Diane and I are Jewish
and celebrate Hanukkah, as does my family; her family
celebrates a completely secular, but still tradition-laden
Christmas. There have been years when we have gone to
my hometown for several days with my entire extended
family—more than twenty people from four generations downing well-oiled latkes, which we still make
from scratch—and afterward drove directly to Diane's
parents' home to be with her family for a few days. It's
like watching your whole life pass before your eyes, with

the best and worst parts all sugarcoated and gift wrapped. (And not just *any* gift wrapping, but color-coded, thematically unique wrapping for each family's presents.)

Don't get me wrong: the highs of these family holiday marathons are some of the best moments in marriage. There is something amazingly powerful about watching your spouse become part of your own family traditions—and truly part of your family. (Actually, my relatives now like Diane better than they like me.) And I'm always amazed by how many of my wife's family traditions I now consider part of my life. In fact, I even got to add one of my own. To blatantly suck up to Diane's family the first year she brought me home, I made a mix tape for her mom, ninety minutes of holiday songs covered by artists I liked. It went over so well that I kept making them. So now my mother-in-law has over thirty hours of holiday music that I programmed. And the first cuing of the holiday mix is as ritualized as the gonzo sugar-cookie decorating or the beverage ballet of my father-in-law's transplendent Irish coffee. My niece Anna has now started making her own competing mix CD.

But along with these wonderful traditions, there is always so much family intrigue: whispers in kitchen corners, siblings huddled off in bedrooms having "private" conversations. Husbands are often clueless about all the details, but even we can sense a pending emotional melee that might force us to rise from our comfy chairs and referee.

I'm often called upon to resolve some standoff between my two younger brothers—or between my mother and sister-in-law, who are capable of grating on each other over the most obscure subjects (including the number of bubbles being produced by the dishwashing liquid). And, of course, I have acquired important duties in my wife's family celebrations. For example, when my nieces and nephews start bouncing off the walls, it's my job to take them outside for a game they call "Uncle Wolf," where I jump out from behind trees and bushes and cars and howl at them, making them shriek with fright and delight and run around until they have burned off the excess sugar and can be safely returned to the nerve-frazzled adult world.

Like many husbands, I am also the designated fetcher. My payback for ignoring all preholiday preparation is to be sent out—again and again—to procure additional supplies. I make a lot of runs for ice and beverages: sodas, milk, juice, and red wine. A lot of red wine.

After all that, the presents can seem a little anticlimactic. In the early years of marriage, it's different. The first year she brings you home, everyone is watching to see if you give her a ring, and during the next few years the family can be charmed by the romantic gift-giving of honeymooning couples. But soon the only gift anyone in the family seems to want is grandchildren. And as soon as one arrives, most gift-giving attention is focused on Tickle Me Elmos, Bumble Balls, Barbie dolls, and Easy-Bake ovens. I've known husbands and wives who, after a while, just stop giving each other gifts—or give token joke gifts. There have been years when Diane and I have been so deluged by holiday deadline pressures, or awful colds, that we have announced moratoria on gift-giving. And, other years, I've dispelled the pressures by just giving Diane the gifts I find for her right after I buy them, so she gets surprise presents all fall.

But I do miss the early days of the grand-gesture gifts, the first diamond ring (which, given my salary at the time, has a stone that can only be seen from certain angles), the first antique watch, that strand of black pearls. And I still can instantly conjure in my mind's eye the year I splurged and gave Diane a Tiffany watch, after which she introduced me to the joys of the carpeted walk-in closet in her parents' guest room.

Y'know, maybe I better get back to my shopping right now.

The Dishwasher Dialogues

Every few weeks my wife attempts to intervene in my troubled relationship with our dishwasher. Like most women trying to get their men to help out more around the house, Diane thinks all I need is a pep talk or a good guilting or a few technical pointers. She still doesn't understand how complex and advanced the problem really is, how much bigger it is than just the dishwasher.

And, of course, she's still in denial about how much of this is her fault.

The Dishwasher Dialogues usually begin when I've finished breakfast and I'm rinsing my dishes in the sink, trying to decide whether to actually deposit them in the dishwasher. At this point I generally call upstairs and ask Diane what I think is a completely reasonable question:

"Are the dishes in the washer dirty or clean?"

She knows the answer to this question. All she has to do is tell me. Instead, she would rather explore why I am unable or unwilling to figure out for myself whether the dishes are dirty or clean.

Diane thinks this is my typical guy way of stalling. This phenomenon is sometimes called "feigned incompetence" (although, interestingly, when women do it, it's usually referred to more sympathetically as "learned helplessness"). But in this case I'm not feigning anything. I mean—really—if I didn't plan to put the dishes in there, why would I call attention to this by asking the question?

Why can't wives just take questions like these at face value? Maybe some men just don't know the difference between rinsed dirty dishes and clean dishes. Or, maybe husbands just come to realize that they and their wives have such a completely different definition of the word "clean" that it's safer to ask than to guess incorrectly.

"They're dirty, okay?" she says, bounding down the steps, coffee sloshing from her "Smart Women Thirst for Knowledge" mug. "So put them in and this time, for once, why don't you actually put in the soap and turn the thing on?"

Well, no, I can't go that far. You see, we've had this dishwasher for more than a year now. And never once have I made it wash dishes. It's stainless steel inside and out, very cool-looking, precision German construction—

the biggest splurge in the whole kitchen. And I'm terri-fied of it.

I'm convinced that if I push the wrong button on the high-tech control panel I will set off a chain reaction that could cause the machine to melt down through the floor and all the way to the earth's core, leaving a trail of suds leading back to me. But before I could even think about turning it on, I would have to finally confront the sphinxlike riddle of the multiple soap trays.

I was perfectly capable of operating our previous dishwasher. I didn't always do it, but at least I *could.* You poured soap powder in the little well, closed the door, and that was that. But in this dishwasher, soap isn't enough. It needs a substance called "rinse agent," which I don't really understand. Is rinse agent to dishes what conditioner is to hair? I tried consulting some literature from the Soap and Detergent Association about this, but when they started talking about the need to "make water wetter" I realized this required a better under-standing of the metaphysics of cleaning than any hus-band is capable of.

More unsettling, however, is the fact that Diane doesn't completely grasp "rinse agent," either. In fact, as she starts showing me just how easy it is to pour the pow-der into the main soap well, I see she's getting a little nervous and having trouble closing that little spring-loaded door, because she knows that once it's locked she will have to show me how to check the "rinse agent."

And she isn't sure herself whether she has been doing it right.

Could it be that all this time our water hasn't been wet enough and our dishes haven't been as spotless as they are supposed to be? And, my God, could that mean that even the Soap and Detergent Association would agree that I am completely justified in my husbandly inability to tell whether they are clean or dirty?

When a man learns that there might be a standard of cleanliness even higher than the one established by his wife and that even she is unsure of how to attain it, he begins to wonder how long other laws of the universe—gravity, for example—will hold. He begins to question certain basic chore dynamics in the household that have existed, well, since that first time he tried to do their laundry.

Ah, I remember the day well. Because after that, nothing in our chore life was ever the same. We had just bought a house together, and it was the first time I had ever done laundry in my own washer and dryer—after years at the Laundromat. I was sitting on the bed, just about done folding our recently joined washables, when Diane started unfolding all the towels I had just folded.

I watched in utter disbelief. She laid them all out flat on the bed, and began giving me a little tutorial on the proper method of folding towels, which involved some form of terry-cloth origami. Instead of folding in successive halves, she wanted one-third of the towel to be folded in from either side. I thought this was ridiculous, but nowhere near as ridiculous as the idea of unfolding already-folded towels—and thereby sending a signal to your newlywed husband that it is more important that a chore be done a certain way than it is for him to actually do it.

I was a little disappointed. I liked the idea of our doing the laundry together and found something kind of sexy about seeing her underwear mingled with mine. But apparently I just couldn't fold anything to her satisfaction.

So now, sometimes, even though I'm not allowed to help, I hang around and chat while she's folding. I even wrote a little song to amuse her (and to distract attention from the fact that I don't ever assist in this enterprise). It's called "Hey, Mrs. Laundry Lady" and has a kind of Mersey-beat feel, sung with a heavy British accent. It goes:

> *Hey, Mrs. Laundry Lady*
> *I love you a load*
> *Hey, Mrs. Laundry Lady*
> *You're hot when I'm warm or cold*

And so on.

Over the years, we've gone through this cycle with every chore she wants me to do. For a while I was doing the bathrooms, but apparently not quite well enough.

For many years I took out the trash, but she decided she really didn't like my choice of trash bags or my tying technique. I've become the husband equivalent of the farmer who is paid not to plant. Yet she still gets annoyed with me for not helping.

So I ask you—what's a husband to do? I've offered to hire someone to help Diane with the chores she won't let me do, but she can't let go of them. When we had a woman helping her clean, Diane would clean the house before she came. So you can see it is actually my wife's fault that I don't help around the house. And the less I do, the more it is her fault.

Unless, of course, this is all a massive rationalization, and an elaborately constructed excuse for male sloth and indolence. But, you know, I doubt it.

Keeping It Up with the Joneses

Guys blab about sex so they don't have to really talk about it. Among my cronies, the unmarrieds carry on about how much they get, while the long-marrieds drop barbs about how much they don't get.

I keep quiet during these discussions. I don't have the guts to ask if what either group is saying is actually true. And I don't want them asking me any questions in return. Why? Because I'm a really bad liar. So I would have to admit to them the scandal of my sex life.

Apparently Diane and I are not keeping up with the national average. According to studies, the average couple in their forties has sex sixty-nine times a year. The average couple in their thirties supposedly does it eighty-six times a year, and in their frisky twenties, one hundred twelve times a year. I have not exactly been keeping written records on my bedroom activities, but I'm pretty sure that if I did, it would prove that we have not been hitting our sexual quota.

It's not that I really believe these sexual statistics. I'd bet that almost everyone in the real married world is below that average. To make the quota of sixty-nine you would have to exceed once a week at home and all the bonus romancing you can do on vacation. (Why is it that sex is so great in hotel beds?) While I'm sure that the researchers who collected this data were very earnest and committed, I think these stats have been padded by a small band of swingers who volunteer for all these surveys (as well as the overclicked delusionaries who don't realize the difference between computer sex and actual human contact).

Also, people lie, especially about sex.

So I will tell you the truth. I'm surprised to be forty-nine years old, sleeping in the same bed every night with a great-looking woman, and not keeping it up with the Joneses.

I'm surprised because I know the slippage in quantity is not in any way related to quality. I was lucky enough to find, smart enough to marry, and loving enough to keep my one true heart. And after two decades together our physical relationship remains remarkably intense. We retain the enthusiasm of honeymooners but have found the proficiency and familiarity that comes only with

practice, practice, practice. (It takes guys a while to figure out what and where everything is.) I know researchers believe that sexual frequency can decline
because of easy accessibility (no thrill of the chase) and
predictability.

My response to this "habituation" theory is the same
one I give my teenage niece Emma, when she periodically e-mails me to tell me how bored she is: If you're
bored, it's because you're boring. The key to unpredictable sex is surprising yourself first, and then your partner. (An absurdly simple example: I recently discovered
that Diane has feet and that those feet have, well, certain sensitivities.)

I also can't blame the downturn on children because,
as my mother subtly reminds me almost daily, we don't
have any. Most couples correlate a slowdown in their sex
lives with the onset of parenthood. I assume they look at
a couple like us and guess that if they were similarly
child-free, they would be having tantric sex dangling
from contraptions attached to the ceiling on a daily, or
at least weekly, basis. But I can tell you: kids are getting a
bad rap here. Feel free to implicate the youngsters in
anything else that bothers you about your life, your marriage, or the future of civilization. But study after study
shows that the biology of aging is the major reason marital relations go from daily to weekly to monthly to, for
some, semiannually.

It's that damn biological clock again. Whenever you

think you've turned off the alarm, you realize you've only hit the snooze button.

I suspect we've just scratched the surface on studying the biology of aging and sexuality. And the number of times couples have sex with each other is not the only issue. What if the frequency of sex with your spouse goes down, but the frequency of sex with, well, yourself, stays the same, or even increases? Until more researchers study these issues—and chart total orgasmic activity—I don't see how we can really know what sexual frequency is average in a marriage at different ages. It would also be interesting to see more research on whether solo sex hurts or helps your relationship with your spouse. I suppose it could lead to more sex together. Or, it could actually inhibit sexual coupling and lead to a separation between pure sexual release and being connected to your partner. That's the last thing that men need, since we're born way too good at the release part but have a steep learning curve on the connecting part.

Sex isn't the only form of physical closeness, of course, it's just the most intense and gratifying. Making each other laugh uproariously can create an afterglow that is nearly postcoital. So can random acts of affection: a friend recently told me how touched she is by the way I sometimes come up to Diane from out of nowhere and kiss her. And I have been known to give non-foreplay back rubs. There are a lot of different ways to be close without sex (and, from what I recall from previous relationships, a lot of ways to have sex without being very close at all).

Make no mistake, I would like to have sex more often. Diane would, too. And it's a myth that frequency only slides downward. In fact, it fluctuates like the Dow, and this year's sexual earnings have been higher than last year's. But we try to recognize and embrace both the rallies and the dips.

I do wonder if we're supposed to be doing anything else about the frequency slowdown—especially since from what I read, the major drop-off is still to come, in our sixties and seventies. I can imagine that a lot of couples just blame each other—or don't talk about it at all, which is the highest form of blaming each other. (I'm especially suspicious of the couples who say they don't have sex anymore and, far worse, that they don't even care.) I think that openly discussing why you don't have sex can be almost as intimate as actually having sex. Sharing responsibility, or even guilt, over missed opportunities is an underappreciated part of the marital balancing act.

And for all my guy friends who think this is about their wives not "putting out," I'll tell you the truth (so Diane doesn't have to).

Sometimes *I* don't put out.

There have been times when Diane took the initiative—which is what all men claim we want our wives to do—and I was either thrown off by not being in control or just too damn mesmerized by some dumb TV show to realize that I was being seduced. Ultimately, I'm gratified that we've been able to maintain a no-fault approach to such mixed messages, and to the entire issue of how often we do it.

In fact, I think one of the sexiest aspects of our marriage is the closeness that comes when we exchange a glance that says it has been too long since we've had sex. When one of us whispers, "I miss you," even though we're sitting right next to each other in a crowded room, we know exactly what to do about it.

Pushing Each Other's Buttons

Moments of revelation don't come often in a marriage, so you have to take them where you can get them. I recently had one such epiphany while sitting in my father-in-law's well-worn leather recliner, which, of course, directly faces the television.

I picked up his remote and started flipping through the channels, eliminating the offerings on channels 2 through 37 in less than ten seconds. Diane claims this quick changing gives her motion sickness but, really, how long do you need to look at a curling match on ESPN 7, or a raccoon peeing on Animal Planet, or *Happy Days* in Portuguese to know that you don't want to watch it? I settled on a rerun of *Everybody Loves Raymond* that I hadn't seen in a while (maybe a week).

Assuming the show could provide up to eight minutes of viewing pleasure before a commercial sent me surfing again, I nestled into the comfy chair.

And then the channel changed.

Stunned, I peered first at the disobedient TV, wondering how it suddenly had sprouted a mind of its own, and then over to the chair on the other side of the reading lamp. There sat my wife, her face suffused with glee. She was wielding a second remote control.

I quickly changed the channel back, then she changed it again. As this escalated, we each got more and more aggressive until we were brandishing the remotes like weapons.

"Boy," I said, "this could get ugly."

Apparently, when my father-in-law bought one of those all-in-one remotes—which works your TV, DVD/VCR, cable box, and the "bagel only" button on your toaster—he decided to let my mother-in-law keep the channel changer that came with the TV as a souvenir. He knew she would never abuse it.

Diane, however, apparently had been waiting her entire married life for her own remote—and the opportunity to push my buttons. As I sat there dueling with her, it occurred to me that the world might actually be improved by inventing a dual remote system. But only if the wifely model—something with more clearly marked buttons, perhaps in pink—became fully operational after the husband had fallen asleep. It could have, say, a snoring sensor in it.

But two live remotes in one marital TV room? Isn't this what defense experts used to call "mutual assured destruction"?

Luckily, we were called to dinner before spraining our thumbs. But the whole incident made me think about just how many marital issues are played out during the seemingly benign act of watching television together—especially since so much movie viewing that once was done in theaters is now done at home. I'm starting to believe that the TV is a window into the soul of your marriage.

Actually, before that remote-control battle I had always thought of Diane and me as being fairly tele-compatible. But that's because I was thinking mostly about programming, where our tastes in TV shows are pretty similar. Yes, she refuses to watch football and I could live my life very happily without Will or Grace. But we mostly agree on what's good, which is convenient because we've always been a one-TV couple, den only. (One of my basketball buddies says that, growing up, his parents had two TVs in their bedroom and watched separate shows with his dad using one of those little white earplugs; he and his wife have the modern equivalent, with his-and-hers TiVo boxes.)

Diane is even sympathetic when I come home from

the picked-over video store and announce we're having another evening of "Best Available Films."

It's in non-programming areas that we run into problems. For example, I feel when you're watching a show you should actually be quiet and, y'know, *watch* it. Diane, however, wants to interact. She likes to talk to the TV and talk to me about what's on the TV—criticizing flaws in plotlines, free-associating on what a character is saying, doing, wearing.

For a while I just slowly turn up the volume. When I finally can't hear over her din, I have been known to shush her. But, I must say, shushing is a risky thing for a husband to do to his wife, and I usually regret it. If I'm lucky, she'll playfully do that zipping motion over her lips or the pantomime key that locks her lips and is dramatically tossed away and won't speak until the next commercial. If I'm unlucky, she'll give me dirty looks all night long until...well, until Jon Stewart, who makes her laugh even when she's mad.

There are also technological problems. While Diane claims she wants her own remote, the truth is that when she's left alone with ours, she invariably pushes the wrong button, or combination of buttons, instantly blanking out the TV screen. And then she proceeds to push pretty much every other button, until the TV screen itself has turned a lovely shade of blue, the VCR is scheduled to tape a show in 2009, and the cable box is set to a channel number that requires a trigonometric solution. Then she calls me on my cell phone, and I can't tell you the number of interviews—or sound sleeps in different time zones—I've had interrupted to help her undo her handiwork.

In her defense, I've had my own technology issues. At the house we lived in for fifteen years we had the old TV and VCR I brought into the marriage—fairly low-tech, but we both knew how to use them and even had jury-rigged a system for taping one show while watching another. When we moved, we bought a new flat-screen TV with a picture-in-picture feature, which I told Diane was worth the extra money because I'd be able to monitor games on the little screen while still watching a show we could both enjoy. Two years later, however, I am still unable to get the little screen up and working—something Diane likes to tell pretty much everyone we meet at cocktail parties. We also got a new DVD/VCR, which is supposedly much more user-friendly, yet it ignores most of my recording requests.

I find this deeply emasculating. But not as emasculating as asking someone for help.

Actually, my biggest complaint about our marital TV viewing involves where we sit. When we were young marrieds, all we could afford in the den was a brown sleeper sofa where you couldn't help but sit close and snuggle. Today Diane has this great leather mission

chair and ottoman, while I slouch on our cozy black
leather couch. She's only six feet away, but I must admit
I kinda miss her. Sometimes during commercials, I'll go
over and visit her, or she'll come visit me.

It's my favorite part of the show.

What Men Talk About
When They're Naked

I often hear wives bemoan the fact that they can't get their husbands to talk to them. They want to know what it would take to hear their men "really open up."

Personally, I think most wives get far more satisfaction from dissing their spouses' communications skills than they could ever derive from hearing what their guys actually have to say. But if you insist on knowing, I will let you in on one of our manly little secrets.

There's one situation where men truly and consistently talk a lot. And that's when they're naked, hanging around in the locker room.

Ever since I was a teenager and got my first chance to sit in a community center's steam room, I've been aware of how differently men speak to one another when they're dressed only in towels. Maybe nudity humbles us, because there's no hiding how far we've strayed from Michelangelo's David-like perfection, and at the same time it frees us. But no matter the reason, the chatter in the locker room has a different quality from the conversations men have, say, when they drink together. There's a terry-cloth truth about these discussions that you just can't get anywhere else.

When I tell my wife about the Chest Hair Dialogues, she's always fascinated and a little jealous. Many of the discussions I have in the locker room are the mundane chats she routinely fails to engage me in at home. She thinks I'm cheating on her conversationally, yakking about politics, business, world affairs, even the weather with naked guys—some of whom I barely know. These are topics I almost never talk about with her, especially as we get past 9:00 PM, when my head begins the "TV nod" like one of those drinking-bird toys.

I also suspect Diane finds it hard to believe I could be that comfortable sitting around naked with *anyone*—because she knows I'm not that way around her. I'm the kind of guy who puts his clothes back on *immediately* after sex, and I haven't taken my shirt off at the beach in, like, thirty years. I don't know why I'm that way (maybe I need a body-image therapist), any more than I understand how I've grown so unself-conscious in the locker room that I no longer bother putting a towel around my waist.

Over the years I've also become something of a student of the sociology of men talking to one another naked. There are several different areas where guys converse, each with its own unwritten rules. The main stage is the locker-and-bench zone, where unrobed conversations take place within earshot of anyone who happens to be nearby. There's a lot of trash talk and one-upmanship, more about sports than anything else—although, interestingly, it's rarely about the sports that the guys just played. It's usually about pro sports that they recently watched (or have an opinion on even if they didn't).

Besides the sports talk, you also hear occasional outbursts of what I call "competitive praise." Two guys, generally fifty-plus, will stand there hurtling compliments at each other—"you look great," "no, no, you look great"—until one has managed to aggressively out-flatter the other. The fact that they're buck naked and demonstrably do not look great just makes it all the more entertaining.

Then there are the whisperers. Although I understand wanting to create a little privacy in this nakedly public setting, their whispering becomes so conspicuous that everyone immediately wonders what they're plotting. And sometimes the wondering is justified. Just a couple of weeks ago a guy with a locker near mine was indicted.

I especially distrust the whisperers because there are

so many other places in the locker room where you can talk more privately. If you and your friends manage to get the steam room or the sauna to yourselves, either is a great place to talk—until an interloper arrives. Then the situation usually becomes too awkward for anyone to say anything.

My favorite place is the whirlpool, which bubbles loudly enough to serve as a watery cone of silence. Our whirlpool is rectangular, so groups of three or four can huddle at either end and, as long as no strangers wander into your whirling space, it feels pretty private. Whirlpool time can be sacred: in our regular basketball group it's not uncommon for guys who are hurt and can't play to show up just for the whirlpool chatter.

I brought up my theory of naked-male communication in the whirlpool recently. One of my basketball buddies immediately said, "Bulls—. Men don't talk to each other any differently when they're naked. In fact, they never talk to each other at all. They only talk *at* each other."

I tried to get him to shut up long enough to agree there was some truth to that (for both men and women), but he was too busy pontificating on why his bachelor life caused him to miss a recent 8:00 AM game.

"The only thing I want to see that early," he said, "is coffee, the paper, and tits."

"I *so* want to be you," shot back one of the married guys.

In all fairness, I've heard naked guys say wonderfully moving things about their wives and families—things they'd probably never say to their wives and families. One of the most amazing moments I ever saw was the outpouring of support for one of our favorite yakkers, a fifty-year-old guy who suffered a stroke after playing the early-morning full-court game. People he barely knew visited him in the hospital, and one club regular—a former pharmaceutical executive who seems to have actually retired to the locker room (he's always there, and nobody has seen him get dressed in almost a year)—started a betoweled fund-raising drive. We paid the injured guy's gym membership for the next few years so he could rehab.

Every once in a while, moving confessions come out in unpredictable ways.

Recently, a guy dressing a few lockers down from mine asked me very casually what my plans were for the evening. I told him my wife was up visiting her parents for a few days.

"So you're a bachelor," he said. And I thought I knew where this was headed. But actually, I was wrong.

"Well, don't do anything stupid while she's away," he implored. "It's not worth it. Believe me, I know."

I found this moment so unexpected and poignant

that, afterward, when I called Diane, I temporarily suspended the court-recognized right of naked-guy privi-
lege and shared the exchange with her.

"It sounds like you guys have your own version of the
Ya-Ya Sisterhood," she said.

I told her I think of it more as the Yada-Yada
Brotherhood. And I'm proud to be a member.

Men Are Such Tools

Whenever I open a toolbox, I hear taunting laughter in my head, like a character in a bad horror movie: *I Know Where Your Vise-Grip Was Last Summer.* And I flash back to the last time I attempted to be handy.

The drain in the bathroom sink was clogged. Technically, I did unclog it—by shattering the entire drainpipe with a monkey wrench. I quickly tried to sop up the mess with paper towels before my handymanliness was called into serious question. But I couldn't keep up with the torrents.

"Hey, um, Steve?" I heard Diane call from the dining room just below me. "Should water be pouring from the light fixture?"

Diane, to her credit, did not laugh at first. But when

our plumber arrived, he could not contain himself. He had one of those musical Jamaican laughs, so infectious that Diane could not resist joining in.

So when we bought a new house, one that needed some work, I didn't waste one second's thought on doing any of it myself. I do realize that do-it-yourself remodeling is now so popular that in some neighborhoods there are as many home-improvement stores as homes. And I have seen the studies suggesting that couples can even be brought closer together by doing such projects themselves. In one survey, fifty-four percent of couples who do home-improvement projects together said they "enjoyed" them. In another survey, thirty-five percent of homeowners said their failed attempts at home improvement had caused "domestic rifts." And almost half described their partners as "useless."

There is, I understand, even a burgeoning handywomen's movement afoot. But Diane is even less do-it-yourself-ish than I am. Which is good, because I'm not sure I could handle being married to someone who is smarter *and* handier than I am.

Yet, while we are both, well, "useless," we are also very opinionated. So we needed a contractor who would let us be completely involved without ever actually getting our hands dirty.

And we actually lucked into the perfect guy: Mike, a fortysomething corporate escapee turned general contractor who can actually use the term "feng shui" correctly but also knows how to rewire an electrical box. He's been great. But we never considered how a guy with a toolbox could get so embedded in our lives and our marriage. After months at a time under our roof, Mike knows way too much about us. He knows what we're like first thing in the morning (me, wide-awake and yapping; Diane, sleepwalking like *The Next Morning of the Living Dead*). He is conversant with our bathroom habits (because he's had to fix our cranky old toilets so many times).

So far, I've seen no evidence that he is using this information for evil. But, then, he doesn't need to. People often complain about hating their contractors. Let me tell you something: It's much more dangerous to *like* your contractor. We've already burned through twice what we originally budgeted, with no end in sight.

Yet I must admit that we've never had so much fun spending too much money and energy on something. It's almost like Diane and I are having our midlife crises together, with all the insane expenditures at least remaining within the marriage and the house. Which is exactly what we hoped for when we bought the place. We guessed correctly that a new house would offer the chance to take on a new set of shared dreams—and the occasional freshly shared nightmare. (There is still a very lonely, inch-wide hole in the granite next to the

kitchen sink awaiting the soap dispenser. After the first
six months, we started telling our friends it was part of
the design concept.)

Making a whole lot of decisions together—even minor ones about window-blind width and handle finish—
is a good test of a relationship, especially since Diane is
very decisive and I am epically ambivalent. I am such an
annoying second-guesser that I should endow a chair at
my alma mater in Indecision Science.

In this case, I deferred to Diane completely on hue.
She indulged my fetish for stainless steel appliances. (If
you want your husband to pay even a moment's attention to remodeling, go stainless in the kitchen: we are
hypnotized by metallic objects.) She was at my side during my endless quest for the Holy Grail of ductless
range hoods. I stood by her when she insisted the grain
on the kitchen cabinets had to be horizontal. And we
hung together during the dusty months of construction
when we slept in the guest loft bed and couldn't unpack
much more than an overnight bag.

In many ways, I am most difficult when a job is finally
completed. It is nearly impossible to get an initial un-
qualified compliment out of me. I am the type of
person who must learn to love almost everything. (Indecisive and hypercritical—just what every woman
wants in a husband.) I look at something Diane, Mike,
and I schemed over for days, and that he created over
weeks or months, and instead of seeing the big picture

of a cool, curved counter or a majestic wall of CDs in the den, I notice only a little splatter of paint or a seam that needs to be touched up. While I am eventually capable of intense appreciation, it is always too late for the egos of others.

Diane believes I do this with Mike because men feel insecure when we can't do home-improvement work ourselves. She says it's not really criticism as much as macho posturing. But it can't be fun for Mike.

In the meantime, it's great to have a new nest. In fact, we've now reached the stage in the home-improvement process that men like the best: I get to cook in the cool, new kitchen, but thank God, I don't have to clean the cool, new house.

Breaking Up Is
Hard to Watch

Suddenly, a lot of couples I know are calling divorce attorneys—including two longtime marriages where I was a member of the wedding party. This could just be a coincidence, or a commentary on my ushering skills. But to me it feels like an epidemic.

When it comes to relationships, men fall into two categories: those who worry too little and those who worry too much. Personally, given the history of male stoicism, I think modern guys can almost never go wrong by overreacting to problems in relationships. It's like emotional affirmative action: it might take a pound of prevention to get an ounce of cure.

Luckily, Diane and I have yet to experience one of those divorces where the couple is so close to you, so intertwined in your life, that the shock waves send an emotional tsunami in your direction. But there's still nothing quite like the first time you hear that someone you know has gotten a restraining order against their spouse or has emptied a joint bank account. Divorces are so much a part of our culture now; we're the first generation to grow up expecting that the marriages of our parents, our peers, and our children would implode at the same unacceptably high rate. So I didn't expect to be so surprised by just how ugly divorces can be.

I also wasn't prepared for how I'd be affected by the astonishing stories you hear from friends once they've stopped their marital spin control. It's not so much the well-kept secrets that shock as the revisionist history of the things you *thought* you already knew. It's the realization that you don't really know anybody until it's too late—and then suddenly you know too much.

My wife and I disagree on why there are so many breakups. My theory is that divorces come in swarms every seventeen years or so like cicadas, brought on in certain marriages by the accumulated personal and professional pressures and the kids getting old enough that you can't use "when the kids get older" as an excuse anymore. Diane views relationships as more fragile than that. Her theory is that in the life of every couple there are "windows of seduceability" for either spouse, and astute partners recognize them and figure out what attention must be paid.

After Diane explained her seduceability theory to me, over dinner at one of our favorite little restaurants, we ordered more wine and proceeded to go through all the couples we know, speculating on who might be at risk in years to come. It is, of course, easier to contemplate the relationships of your friends than to actually discuss your own fears. Or, maybe the discussion about other people's marriages is really about your own.

I used to be almost ambivalent about divorce— probably because I've never been through one myself. I somehow avoided that "starter marriage" many of my friends (and my wife) had in their twenties—most of which appeared to end pretty amicably.

But divorce is much more painful and resonant when it's a relationship that has survived into your thirties and forties. There are kids involved this time, and that's just brutal. I sometimes feel as if I should be piling these children into the car and taking them to the zoo for, say, a year until their parents get through the worst of their acting out. And there's money and property to split up. The biggest things my peers divided during the 1980s divorces were record collections.

But, ultimately, it's the less predictable aspects of twenty-first-century divorce that so unnerve me. For example, I'm seeing more relationships where it's actually the wife's affair that leads an unstable marriage to finally blow up. I realize it's sexist of me to be surprised by this, but I still am.

I'm also amazed at what absolute wrecks separating and divorcing husbands are—and how hard it is for these guys to find anyone who will care about their feelings. I'm not trying to take sides in these divorces. But while both halves of a couple either make or break a marriage, people are not accustomed to paying much attention to the guy's emotions. When men realize it's over, they are often like sodas that have been shaken for years and are finally opened.

You should hear the way men talk about the breakup of their marriages during private moments. What they have to say can be astonishingly honest, and often kind of brilliant. It's all the stuff they never said when it mattered—all the things they were afraid were going wrong, but were too afraid to talk about, because saying anything out loud might make it too real. It's their guilt about the stuff they know they shouldn't have done, but did anyway, before and after their marriages hit the wall.

In most cases, their wives (or ex-wives) will never hear a word of this. It is simply too late for these insights.

This breaks my heart, because the longer I'm married, the more I feel like a cockeyed relationship optimist. I firmly believe that most troubled marriages are

just a few hard-earned insights away from stability. (I'm
the one who always answers "yes" to *"Can This Marriage
Be Saved?"*) To me, there's nothing worse than a life-
changing realization that arrives just *after* the nick of
time. Especially because, unlike those marriages that
failed when we were in our twenties, I'm not sure how
many of these guys will be able to use these insights to
find love again.

While the divorce rate has been stable for a while,
rates of remarriage have gone down, as have the proba-
bilities that a second marriage will work out. And there
is also a marked difference between the way men and
women handle divorce. In a stunning piece of research
published not long ago, it was revealed that divorced
men commit suicide nearly ten times more often than
divorced women. But divorced women don't commit
suicide any more often than married women do. This
information shocks but somehow doesn't surprise.
Divorced women know how to take care of one another.
Psychologically, divorced men are like all men—away
from work they barely know how to take care of
themselves.

I think women often assume that long-married guys
will be jealous of their peers who are suddenly "freed,"
which is why they often fear that divorce can be conta-
gious in groups of couple friends. While I have noticed
great solidarity among men who bitch about their
marriages or even stray from them, I've seen very

little closeness among men whose marriages are actually over.

I don't envy these guys their freedom one bit. I worry for them. And I am committed to doing whatever it takes not to join them.

My Hair, My Self

My wife pulled me aside very conspiratorially during a recent weekend with my in-laws. She and her two sisters, she said, needed some "private time." They were wondering if I could do something with the kids—my nephew and three nieces—for a couple of hours. I figured they needed to discuss the imploding marriage of Diane's older sister. So I took all four kids to the movies and then to John's Plain & Fancy Diner, where a slice of pizza somehow ended up on my nephew Eli's back.

When we returned, I wandered into the kitchen to find out why the sisters needed all this private time. Before anyone said a word, I knew.

They had different hair.

Their four hours had been spent sipping champagne and giving one another highlights.

Now, most guys wouldn't have minded this. They would have appreciated the finished product and probably enjoyed conjuring up the provocative image of three babes—and these three are—guzzling bubbly and doing one another's hair, perhaps in various stages of undress.

But I was annoyed. Though not for the reasons you'd think. As the "cool uncle," I actually enjoy taking the kiddos out. I was annoyed because I've been lobbying my wife to stop coloring her hair. I'm one of the minority of husbands who actually like silver-haired women. You'd think this would be a welcome fetish in any marriage, which just shows how much I know. Turns out, women do their hair for each other, not for us.

But, more than that, I was annoyed because their afternoon just reinforced how much fun women can have with their hair. I'm jealous. For men, hair is a deadly serious business—as fun as an ingrown toenail.

Let's face it: while women are expected to experiment with their hairstyles (sometimes to the point of abstract expressionism), men generally get one or two hairstyles in their lives. In many cases, that second hairstyle is an involuntary—and mortifying—one.

My best friend started losing his hair in his early twenties. I didn't know how he felt about it because it's one of the only subjects we have never *ever* discussed. But I recently asked him what it was like for him to lose what I'd guess has been about one-fourth of his hair.

Normally chatty, he responded tersely, "Losing my hair feels like the antithesis of losing my virginity." When asked to elaborate, he refused, mumbling something about "denial even of the denial."

Another friend says the real problem is that hair is the only aspect of male body image that can change drastically and involuntarily at a point in your adult life when you think you know pretty much how you look. So it's the change, the way you no longer look like yourself to yourself, that gets to you. You spend your whole life short or tall, with a big nose or a small penis. Weight rises and falls, but that's generally your fault and in your control. The grim hair reaper comes when least expected.

I have been damn lucky in the hair department, inheriting a very thick mane from my father's side of the family. When my peers started losing their hair in their twenties, I actually decided to grow mine longer—and discovered it had a life of its own, full of dramatic waves and flourishes. Then I met Diane, who liked my hair long and actually encouraged me to grow it even longer. My hair soon became my most identifying and noteworthy physical characteristic.

Now people actually stop me on the street, or corner me in the elevator to tell me they like my hair or ask who cuts it. And my haircuts have been known to generate commentary among family, friends, and guys at the gym. My wife usually thinks it's been cut too short. My mother always says she thinks it's still too long. And then she says it again.

To me, length is no longer the issue. Over the past few years, my hair has gone pretty much completely gray. I suppose this would bother some fortysomethings. Me, I'm happy to have this much hair of any hue. I still look like myself to myself in gray hair. Because of my size— I'm a big-boned six-foot-two and have been since my early teens—I've always looked older than I am anyway. So far, I've been able to handle the increase in people referring to me as "sir." I'll see how I react the first time someone says I look "distinguished." (That's a comment gray-haired men get much more often than gray-haired women, a gender prejudice Diane occasionally—and justifiably—rails about.)

Since men take their hair seriously, we have very involved relationships with those who cut it. I've been with Charles for nearly two decades. Although he has, in general, supported my hair goals, he once suggested I rinse my gray out. Glaring at him, I told him we would never speak of this again.

Recently, however, I had my first real hair worry. Guys with long thick hair shed, just like sheepdogs. But now there's more hair than ever in my brush, or being picked off my sport coat by my wife.

This is not something I can complain about to my male friends—especially those less hair-fortunate than I. And whining to Diane doesn't help, either. First she claimed she didn't notice it. Then she said she didn't care if all my hair fell out; she would still love me.

I can't decide which answer is worse—or less true.

Perhaps this is my punishment for being, yes, a little hair-smug all these years. My theory, however, is that this slight hair-thinning is temporary, caused by my low-carb, 3-D House of Meat Diet Plan. And as soon as I have the courage to go off the diet (and gain all the weight back in two weeks), I'll be fine. But, in the meantime, I went to Charles for a follicular physical.

He stroked my hair—not to calm me, but to closely examine my scalp. He said I was fine, and that he felt lots of new little sprouts down there. I need to believe him. I need to believe that something extraordinary is possible.

You Can Look but
You Better Not "Track"

We're sitting in a restaurant having a nice dinner, and my wife looks terrific. Suddenly, over her shoulder, I can see another woman walking toward our table. At the moment, it is safe to look at both of them. Diane is in a clingy red blouse (she's going through a red phase), her bangs are dancing around her eyes, and she has a sexy smile. The other woman is wearing—well, at this point it doesn't really matter what she's wearing. She's a woman coming into my field of vision. And as a man, my genetic predisposition is to look. At least for a second.

How long you look beyond that second may determine how long you will stay married. If your wife pays any attention to you at all, she can tell when your eyes are no longer focused on her face and conversation.

Most wives, I believe, will forgive these subtle eye movements. Every guy does them. And, frankly, so do women—who notice men and, well, *everybody.*

But if you begin to move your head, even just slightly, you are taking a big risk. In fact, at this moment, it is not really safe to even look for the salt or signal for the waitperson. You must keep your neck locked at all costs.

Because if you begin "tracking"—that is, turning your head to follow the woman walking past—you're dead. Once you've been caught tracking, your wife knows you're a guy who tracks. In the unwritten rules of marriage, you've crossed a line. From that point on, she'll be watching to see whatever you're watching.

Almost everybody tracks. But nobody wants to be married to someone who tracks right in front of them.

The only exception is if someone walks by who is so outrageously dressed that the "train-wreck rule" applies. We are all allowed to look at train wrecks, car crashes, and women in restaurants dressed only in their underwear. It's an activity that brings couples together. In fact, smart husbands covertly signal that the train-wreck rule is in effect by nudging their wives or cocking their heads toward the sight to be seen. Together. In the parlance of traffic reporting, this is called a "gaper alert." These gaper alerts can save marriages by creating shared laughter.

I started thinking about tracking at a 76ers game. I was there with a friend who, like me, is very happily married. It was just us two guys, so there was no reason why we shouldn't track to our hearts' content, especially because some of the women at professional basketball games are really only there to be tracked, dressed in their best and most revealing *Girls Gone Wild* outfits.

Still, when my friend started tracking to the point where his head almost did an *Exorcist* spin, I found myself becoming self-conscious, maybe even a little judgmental. When he went to get more nachos and beers, I wondered what was going on.

I realized that I don't ever track women like that, even when I'm just around other men. I don't want them to catch me looking, either. I've conditioned myself to do this over the years, the same way one is conditioned not to use the f-word in front of children. It's like I don't want to be the stereotypical "normal guy" even though I am allowed to be him.

I suspect this all goes back to my childhood and family vacations at the beach. My dad, like most men of his era, did a lot of gaping as bathing suits got more and more daring. And my poor mom—the only woman in a family of a father and three sons—would often openly comment about how "built" the women were that he was looking at, as if talking like one of the guys would make her feel less left out. I never wanted to put any woman through that.

But, ultimately, it doesn't matter whether a husband is moving his eyes until there's nothing left but the whites of them, or tracking so obviously that he gives himself whiplash. The real issue is: What does looking at other people mean in a marriage? Is it a "gateway drug" that leads, eventually, to touching? Or, is looking actually just a healthy way of immunizing yourself against touching? The problem, of course, is that looking can either be a symptom or a treatment. Sometimes it is both. And other times it is neither: it is simply a normal appreciation of a natural phenomenon that just happens to have a great butt.

Some wives may think that looking at other women, or tracking, is all about temptation. I don't really believe that. Temptation is something much more personal and private and convoluted, and I suspect it only gets associated with an actual "other person" pretty late in a deeply internal process. Looking and tracking are much more Pavlovian than that. At my regular half-court basketball game, if a woman wanders from the workout area onto the far end of our court, the guys gape even though most of them can't even see that far without their glasses (or with their prescription goggles). So they can't really tell if the woman is twenty or ninety or attractive or an alien life-form.

Wives shouldn't be bothered by this any more than they should be bothered by channel surfing. It's not about sex. It's about the complete and utter distractibility of men. We have trouble staying focused on anything for very long—regardless of whether it's a TV show, something you're trying to tell us, a song on the radio, some really, really important thing you're *still* trying to tell us, or simply a pretty woman walking by. Just give us a moment, and we'll switch back to our regularly scheduled wife, already in progress.

Clothes Unmake the Man

Before we go out for the evening, my wife checks her hair, makeup, and outfit for the ninety-eighth time. The checklist astronauts use prior to launching the space shuttle is shorter than the one Diane uses before we can head out for the movies. And I'm still amazed at some of the items on the list. I had no idea how much effort it took to make sure your breasts are placed evenly in your bra.

The last thing on Diane's list is to evaluate what I'm wearing. Unless we are going somewhere very dressy—black-tie affair, funeral, black-tie funeral—I am wearing what all fortysomething men wear: relaxed jeans, relaxed shirt, relaxed shoes with relaxed socks, relaxed boxers. Sometimes I'll add a relaxed blazer.

And when she sees me dressed in all these baggy,

rumpled clothes—looking like a six-foot-two shar-pei—
she is unable to cloak her disappointment.

"You know," she says, "I thought I married a man who
dressed! Whatever happened to that guy? I can't even remember the last time you wore a pair of pants where I
could see your butt!"

I am glad that after twenty years of marriage, my wife
still wants to see my butt. (I still very much want to see
hers; in fact, she's examining it right now in the full-
length mirror—check!) And I am sorry that Diane feels
she is the victim of some sort of sartorial bait-and-switch.
But it's not my fault that as couples age, women tend to
pay more attention to their appearance while men pay
considerably less to their own. I did not set out to become so, um, relaxed in my personal standards of dress.
I am a victim of my society.

Throughout history, men were forced by their bosses
and wives to dress a certain way. Then in the mid-1980s,
a variety of forces conspired to change all that. (This
was around the time that Diane and I met, so it's her
bad luck that we fell in love just as the very fabric of
men's fashion was going baggy.) There was the fitness
craze, which made workout clothes more respectable
outside the gym. There was rap culture, which made
sweat suits and long, formless shorts *très* fashionable.
There was "casual Friday," which ultimately destroyed
the need to dress up even for work.

This all led to that watershed moment in men's

fashion: the invention of casual clothing—khaki pants with a stretch waistband, jeans with extra "comfort" built into the waist and crotch. Increasingly, male casual clothing became "supersized," until there was no longer any small, medium, or large—just extra large, extra extra large, and "tarp."

Sociologists may ponder for years how all these trends came together, but ask any man and he'll tell you why. To guys, it all amounts to the same thing: easier access for scratching.

(We know we're not supposed to scratch in public. It's unseemly. But we can't resist. We're men. It's what we do.)

As much as I hate to admit it, there are times when I share Diane's disappointment. I sometimes ask myself, How did I become a guy for whom "dressing up" means wearing black jeans and an unfaded T-shirt under an untucked oxford?

One part of the problem, I think, is that while wives consider fashion a statement of who they are, men view fashion as who they *aren't.* To most men, clothing is just a uniform—nothing much better than a prison jumpsuit. Whether a guy wears a suit and tie every day, or baggy pants and an oversize T-shirt, it's still a uniform, which is why men would buy twenty of whatever it is and wear the same outfit every day if they could. (Actually, many of us wouldn't care if we wore the same exact clothes every day. Luckily, men are the only animals that can't smell themselves.) Eventually, a man is known by his uniform and feels uncomfortable wearing anything else.

Diane offers a solution to this: If men need to wear the same thing every day, why can't it be a tuxedo? Every man, regardless of girth, age, or stature, looks his absolute best in a tuxedo. Maybe if I wore a tux once a month—even just around the house, while watching TV and scratching myself—I could earn the right to dress casual the rest of the time.

But that's not what Diane wants. She yearns for the stylish guy she remembers from our courting days. Although she has conveniently forgotten some of my more questionable choices—my best friend's mother-in-law had my red socks airbrushed out of their wedding-party portrait—she is correct in remembering that wearing attractive clothes once mattered more to me. And she is still hoping that we can return to what she refers to as "the salad days" of our sartorial relationship.

What wilted our salad days? I suppose there are men who stop dressing well when they feel they no longer have to, since they have already successfully hunted and gathered an appropriate spouse. But that wasn't the case for us at all. I still court my wife in almost every way but fashion. I think it may literally be about how many days I eat salad. Men who, like me, fight weight gain often come to despise all clothes, especially those that actually make contact with our bodies. Most guys, however, will start dressing better again when they lose weight—and I did do that for a while. But once you've loved and lost and gained a couple of times, you realize it's easier just to maintain one drapey wardrobe.

This system has worked for me but not for Diane. So recently I've started to just let her dress me for certain social occasions. I simply ask, flat out, what she would like to see me in. Asking this question can have its benefits. Diane recently convinced me to wear this chocolate-brown suit I bought a couple of years ago and, literally, wore only while it was being marked up by the tailor. For some reason, it suddenly appealed to me, so now I wear it on every dressy occasion. But getting Diane involved in these choices can also be dangerous, especially during warm months. Diane thinks that all men look like toddlers in summer clothes: the baggy shorts, the huge T-shirts. We might as well be licking big round lollipops. So her solution is that I should wear tight black jeans all year round—even in the dead of August—just so she can feel less mortified.

On those days, when I get home and scratch myself, I really feel I've earned it.

Drives Me Crazy

I really love driving with my wife, which is why I get upset when she tells me how much she hates driving with me.

She doesn't say this all the time. Over the years, we've spent a lot of quality time together in the car: just the two of us on the open road, with plenty of time for talk, big and small, powered by our favorite CDs and way too many caffeinated beverages. In fact, we have better-developed husband and wife roles in the car than anywhere else. I am always the driver. (I can't stand being driven: If I died in a car crash with someone else at the wheel, I'd kill myself.) And Diane, who prefers to be driven, has anointed herself "The Master Passenger." This means it's her job to keep the conversation lively in order to keep the driver awake. Because of this, we've had many breakthrough conversations in the car. I think she saves up topics.

Since the car has become such a nurturing environment—sometimes it's like being in a great therapy session, and other times it's like being serviced by a geisha from Mensa—I am always surprised when the conversation turns frosty. Which it does with surprising regularity on one subject: directions.

In the war between the sexes, driving directions are the ultimate minefield. Whenever I hear the sound of Diane unfolding a map or paging through a MapQuest printout, or I see her lower her glasses on her nose to read my hand-scrawled directions, I know we're about to head into Car Paradise Lost.

The conversation generally starts when we are approaching an exit or juncture that isn't in our directions, and I'm not sure which way to go. Diane often doesn't realize I am feeling indecisive, and then I get angry when she doesn't already know the answer to a question I haven't yet asked her.

Every once in a while, a husband becomes wifely and expects *his* mind to be read.

Then I start getting a little panicky and begin speaking in That Tone. You know the one. And suddenly the decision about whether or not to turn becomes a microcosm of our entire relationship. It turns into a referendum on who I trust more: her or myself. She has the map, but I'm the one at the wheel with the instinct that something isn't right. And frankly, Diane, like many women, is better at making sure we follow driving directions than she is at actually seeing where we're going. (Just so you don't think I'm taking gender-based cheap shots, this was recently proven in a study published in the *Annals of the Association of American Geographers.*)

This crisis ends either with my turning, or not turning, or actually stopping the car on that little island of indecision that highway makers build at each exit where guys like me can park and bark at our wives—who are so worried now that a truck is going to plow into us that they've long since forgotten the original question.

Eventually, we go the wrong way and make three U-turns, while I ignore Diane's pleas that I pull in to a gas station and ask for directions. Then I go to a gas station, where I refuse to write down the directions the guy gives me, because men are too cool for that. Finally, we have to call whoever we are heading to see, and he gives us new directions, sometimes even talks us in on the cell phone like passengers who had to take over flying the plane: "Okay, that's it, make the next left, pull up past that mailbox, and we're the house with the guy on the front porch yelling at you on his phone."

But, except for that, we have a really great time driving together. Except for one other thing. Diane hates the way I drive in the city. The honking and the hand gestures—which I consider part of any normal driver's vocabulary of communication—she finds aggressive and dangerous. She leaves newspaper stories out for me about people maimed or executed by drivers they cut in front of or made obscene gestures to. She says she doesn't want to be a road-rage widow (which actually sounds like a good name for a country song).

Oh, and she also hates the general cleanliness level in the car, which is usually just one step above the bottom of my gym bag. We drive a pretty unexceptional car—late-model, black Toyota Camry, perfect for FBI agents on a budget—and since we live in the city, we don't bother repairing minor dings and scrapes. So, in my defense, even when the car is sparkling, it still doesn't look that great. (To a husband, that's a defense.)

But, except for the directions thing, the alpha-male driving habits, and the Diet Pepsi bottles and Starbucks cups piling up in the backseat, we love being in the car together. That is, as long as we can agree about what's on the radio. While we sometimes bring CDs, we stick to the radio until we're out of range of anything listenable. I usually try to start with NPR. But after about five minutes, Diane starts chanting "good times, good times" from that spoof on *Saturday Night Live,* until I agree to change the station and find her a Led Zeppelin song. To her, that's the ultimate car music.

I could debate this musicologically—and in fact I have, since being in the car, at the mercy of whatever comes on the radio, often does inspire me to musicological discourse. Diane plays along until I ask her to make a Top 10 list of themed songs (such as, "Top 10 Songs about Bad Drivers"). Then she looks at me and asks, "What is it with boys that they always want to make Top 10 lists? Girls have better things to do with their time."

And then each of us hopes the other one remembered to bring the CDs. But only if they're the right CDs. Led Zeppelin, Elvis Costello, Miles Davis, or Al Green are always right for her. Anything else, it's a crapshoot.

So, except for all these things, my wife and I love driving together. And now that I've publicly questioned her map-reading, I think I have a pretty good idea what topics The Master Passenger will be bringing up on our next big drive.

Go Fish

During the early years of marriage, my primary leisure activity was being married. It was all so new and different. I was still astonished at always having a date.

Diane was perfectly happy to have an attentive husband but eventually she started to wonder what was wrong with me—especially when the weather would get warm, and regular guys were out doing regular guy things.

Of course, I took this to mean that I should find something new for us to do together: tennis, yoga classes, chess. We did play tennis once (at one of those embarrassing love-nest hotels with the heart-shaped tubs and the his-and-her snorkels). We did try yoga, briefly (I was the only guy in the class, and the only student who had to sit down to bend at the waist). And we did play some chess, until I realized she was just toying with me to teach me how to be more Machiavellian in a particular work situation (since I later learned she could kick my ass in three moves whenever she wanted).

Eventually, Diane admitted that she actually didn't want to find a new activity for us to do together. She wanted me to find a new activity for us to do—*not* together.

"You know, you need a hobby," she said, laughing at the sound of the word. It seemed like an artifact from our pre-VCR childhoods, when boys were encouraged to play with model trains so they wouldn't discover sex. "Something to get you out of the house. Go . . . fish!"

While I liked the concept of fishing, I did find it a little odd that it was her idea, not mine. After all, don't regular guys fish to get away from their wives? If your wife tells you to go fish, isn't that somehow defeating the whole purpose?

At the time, though, I was mostly really glad she hadn't tried to make me golf. There are basically two kinds of men: golfers and fishermen. Golf is clubby, social, competitive, classist. Fishing is more solitary and egalitarian (although fly-fishing can be a tad golfy) and is competitive only when my brothers and I do it. Golf is for strivers and fishing is for yearners, but each activity is profound and pointless in its own way.

I grew up in a divided family. My Pop-pop was an avid

golfer, while his brother—my father's favorite uncle—
was a fisherman. This explains why one of Dad's favorite
places to fish was the pond at the local country club.

I inherited the lunker gene and, as a kid, loved fishing with my father. But after I moved away from home I
stopped. Diane would see my old fishing stuff jammed
into a corner of our car trunk and wonder why I never
touched it. The truth is that I wasn't sure where, or even
how, to fish on my own, without my father. And I felt a
little unmanly admitting that, even to myself.

So on that warm summer day when Diane told me to
go fish, I was reduced to looking in the yellow pages for
a bait shop. I drove to Bob's Bait and Tackle and bought
a license, a rod and reel, and enough lures so I could
lose the first twenty and still have something to fish with,
and then sheepishly asked Bob where I should go fishing. He sent me to a place a half hour away from our
home in Philadelphia, reachable by a dirt road behind
some railroad tracks, where the Schuylkill roars across a
thirty-foot waterfall. When I got there it was early evening and the mayflies were hatching. They hovered in
the air like tiny alien spacecraft, their pale-green wings
fluttering against the rosy sunset sky. As I sat tying my
line, on a rock just above the falls, fish were lunging out
of the water at the mayflies and all manner of birds were
swooping in for them. It was fishing heaven.

I fished until it was so dark that I couldn't even see
the bass I was reeling in. (Taking hooks out using the

"touch system" is not the smartest idea.) And then I did something my dad never would have done—even if the technology had been available. I called Diane on my cell phone.

She was incredulous: why would I violate the blissful peace of my riverside solitude by making a phone call? Because I wanted to let her know that I understood. I understood that she wasn't just trying to get me away from her so she could write. She was trying to help me get away from myself—which is much harder. Figuring out how to be alone was an important step forward in our being together.

Later on, after I had started fishing more regularly, we talked about the phenomenon of the fishing or golf "widow." This fear of being "widowed" in your marriage, or being in competition with your spouse's avocation, is complex. I can only imagine what it's like when couples have the same hobby. I don't mean the situations where one spouse gets involved with something and the other decides to get involved as well, as a preventive measure (to make sure the husband isn't meeting any hot babes at the model railroad show). I mean couples who are, say, both good tennis players or golfers, so they play against each other—those "till sudden death do us part" marriages. While I'm sure there are some joys attached to such situations, I'd imagine the worst part is that you have no one to come home to and exaggerate about how well or how badly you played.

There was a moment, when I first started fishing again, that I thought Diane might want to join me. We were in our favorite place in the world, in the Sangre de Cristo Mountains in New Mexico, where a good friend has a cabin in an old private hunting compound. When we're there, she reads while I fish. But instead of having to go miles from home to fish—or even days away, like the Canadian trip where I caught, and then released, the massive northern pike in my all-time favorite fishing picture—I have only to walk about a hundred yards from the cabin to find all the trout I could possibly catch. The property has three stocked lakes and private access to the Pecos River.

After days of watching from the cabin window as I fished, Diane came out to join me. I gave her a lesson, and she quickly caught a fish. But, while she occasionally talks about trying it again, what I think she's really hooked on is the idea of seeing me fish, enjoying the intense satisfaction of being alone with myself.

It is a powerful feeling to know someone wants you to have that kind of contentment. It is, in fact, exactly the opposite of widowhood.

What's Love Got to Do with It?

I'm sitting courtside with my basketball cronies, sweaty and stinking after six arduous half-court games. So, of course, the conversation turns to romance.

Valentine's Day is looming, and we're talking about how couples celebrate the holiday of the heart if, in fact, we still celebrate it at all. We're also discussing, generally, how we maintain romance in our marriages.

One of the guys, long married with a bunch of kids, launches into a very sensitive, thoughtful sermonette about how Valentine's Day is a completely invented and imposed card-company holiday, and that it's much more important to show your wife you love her in little ways, every day. Doing the dishes, cleaning up.

We're all very touched by his words, until someone

asks how often he actually commits these random acts of marital kindness.

"Almost never," he admits. "Just because I realize this is the key to a successful marriage—at least, my wife keeps telling me it is—doesn't mean I'm that great at it. But making a big fuss on Valentine's Day can backfire, too. One year I bought her an $80 bouquet and she yelled at me for wasting all that money."

So with all this knowledge and insight, what will he be doing this Valentine's Day?

"I'm getting her something nice," he says. "I'm not stupid."

At least he's trying. Another member of the half-court crew admits he ignores days of romance altogether. Married twenty-three years, he can't remember the last time he did anything for his wife for Valentine's Day, or even her birthday—although he is hoping "to get my butt in gear to at least remember our twenty-fifth anniversary."

He says the key to his marriage is "I treat my wife wonderfully every day, and she, too, treats herself wonderfully every day."

I'm in an unusual situation when it comes to Valentine's Day. I met Diane at a Valentine's Day dance party, the "Passion Bash." It was pretty much love at first sight—or at least first dance—and exactly a year later, I proposed to her on the steps of the club where the party had been held. "My Funny Valentine" is our song. So we're fairly romantic about Valentine's Day, because in many ways it rivals our anniversary. We always go out for a nice dinner. We buy each other flowers. We give gifts only if we come across—or create—something that is meaningful and romantic. (Diane has given me poems and drawings. One year I actually sculpted two small clay hearts, although they looked like something made by the kid at camp who is bad at sports.) We break out the good wine, the good candles, and the good underwear (which, for men, usually just means clean, un-ripped, fresh boxers).

Yet, the truth is, despite its significance in our rela-tionship, we still have completely different ideas about Valentine's Day. Diane always thought it was a ridiculous contrivance. Her most powerful image of the holiday was a bus ride on Valentine's Day eve, coming home from her first job out of college. All the women on the bus were laden with stuffed animals, heart-shaped boxes, all the stuff they were going to lavish on their boyfriends and husbands. And all they did during the entire ride was complain about how their significant others "better damn well" have presents for them this year. To her, the entire holiday was invented to turn men into dogs who jumped through hoops.

I, on the other hand, have always romanticized Val-entine's Day. Maybe too much. I can recall many years when I was just a wreck because I had no valentine. To me, it was worse than not having a date on New Year's

Eve. Actually, the only reason there was even a "Passion Bash" where I could meet Diane was because I and three other single friends were so desperate for dates that we decided to pool our misery and host a party where we might troll for love.

I still think one of the best things about Valentine's Day is that it makes people reconsider the importance of love and romance in long-term marriages. There's nothing wrong with a spouse being reminded periodically how miserable life can be without love.

Yet, while most men aren't vocal about it, love is still what we want from marriage. And neither flowers, nor candy, nor sex, nor even doing the dishes is a substitute for love. What should a wife want for Valentine's Day? And what should her husband have the courage to give her? The first, and still the most basic, sign of affection between two people—and an act that gets less and less attention as relationships mature. A kiss. A big wet one.

Diane often tells me she hears more and more women gripe that the biggest thing missing from their marriages is kissing. Apparently, a lot of men don't even kiss their wives during sex—which is like scoring a run without tagging first base. How often men kiss—really kiss—their wives is probably more important than the frequency of sex or how often they help with the dishes.

Of course, there's nothing wrong with making out, having sex, *and* washing the dishes (although maybe not in that order). But I would tell my basketball buddies, and any other men out there listening, your wives really aren't wondering why you've stopped bringing them flowers. They wonder why you've stopped kissing them.

So this Valentine's Day, save yourself eighty bucks and, instead, go home and make out with your wife. You'll be glad you did.

Take Two Famil**EZE** and
Don't Call Me in the Morning

It begins the moment you're married and it never stops—even after you're dead.

It's the competition over whose family gets more time with you, as a married couple. And, believe me, it's a competition that nobody really wins, which is amazing when you consider how much time and energy is spent keeping score.

Whose family gets you for which major holidays? Whose family gets more "spontaneous" drop-ins for dinner? Who has more access to the grandchildren?

And, of course, at whose family plot will you be spending eternity?

"How do you love me?" some parents may ask, with pleading eyes or telephone sighs. "Let me count the days."

By the way, I don't blame families for feeling possessive of their married children's time. I understand those
feelings completely. While I adore my wife's family,
sometimes when I'm having fun with them I feel as if
I'm cheating on my own kin. I doubt my in-laws could
ever understand just how guilty I occasionally feel because I like them as much as I do. And I understand my
own parents' pain that they had to let go and share my
brothers and me with our spouses' clans.

I think most people assume that their family will be
more prominent in the marriage. I know I did. We grew
up minutes from my father's parents, whom we saw
every Friday night for dinner and on all holidays—while
visiting with my mom's family much less. And all our
lives we saw people marrying into our family and getting
sucked into its orbit.

Then I met Diane, whose family was also accustomed
to being the center of the galaxy.

Since we got married in late October, we had been
back from our honeymoon for about two days when
we had to begin negotiations over the most competitive run of holidays on the calendar—Thanksgiving
through New Year's. It's times like these when you wish
you could hire a "relationship agent." What you're looking for is the ability to leverage any concessions against
the tricky spring holiday gauntlet, which runs, depend-
ing on your religion, from Easter or Passover through
Mother's and Father's Days and, since a lot of parents

got married in June (as ours did), a set of competing wedding anniversaries.

Smart relationship agents would also include language about high school reunions, which may require a bonus trip home every five years. They might also broach the touchy subject of any family summer vacationing, which is actually more of a futures market. In reality, parents are less invested in vacationing with you than in securing valuable options on time-shares with their as-yet-unborn grandchildren.

Of course, we hadn't thought about any of this—we were still writing thank-you notes. (And when I say "we," I mean Diane.) We let it all unfold naturally and, for several years, geography helped keep everything manageable. Because the drive to Diane's hometown took eight grueling hours and her siblings were scattered, the family had a tradition of getting together up there only twice a year, but for a week each time. My parents lived closer, but still too far away for a day trip. We saw them much more often than hers, but always in short bursts.

Naturally, each family wanted what the other had. Diane's parents wished they saw their daughters more. My parents were jealous of the blocks of time we spent with her family. But we had it pretty easy. We were dealing with two intact, relatively sane families, and because our parents grew up in different faiths, there weren't even any religious holidays to dispute.

As our siblings got married, we adjusted to their holiday negotiations, and all seemed under control. Then Diane's parents moved closer to us than my parents, about an hour away. Actually, they moved around the corner from Diane's younger sister and their first two grandchildren; proximity to us was just a coincidence. But Diane's extended family was suddenly easier to visit than mine. (They were only 46.22 miles away, compared to 112.75 miles—but who's counting?)

On my side, my younger brother and his wife had the only grandchild (thus far), my nephew Jake. But as their Manhattan apartment was not a natural family gathering place, Diane's family was leading on the cosmic scorecard: four grandkids to one, and a more accessible venue.

Then my father died. His loss was devastating in so many ways, but there's one I've never admitted out loud—an aching feeling that it marked the end of any "competition" between the families, and mine had somehow lost. And, whether Diane's family ever felt this way, the truth is, for the past decade, they have dominated my married life. I am very close to my mother and two brothers, and treasure the holidays we spend with our extended family. I call my nephew in New York every Saturday after his basketball or baseball game. But I see my in-laws more often than my own blood.

I know this kills my mom. I hear it in the way she sighs

when I phone her from Diane's parents' house. But what I don't think she understands is that it kills me, too.

Damn, I wanted my family to win. At least it was a defeat without bloodshed. And over time, the families have actually grown closer. My side of the family now comes to Diane's family Thanksgiving.

And we've actually added an ambitious new tradition—something Dad always dreamed of. For the past ten years, both clans have gotten together for an entire week at my family shore house.

Yes, that's right. All of us. On purpose.

Diane refers to this annual enclave as the "Ayres & Fried Family Beachfest and Food Fight." But with seventeen family members and three dogs living in close quarters, it's more like a reality TV show.

The annual event—which I organize through relentless e-mails—combines traditions of both families really well. From my side you get the long walks, the gold-rush-style sea-glass hunts, the seafood extravaganzas, and the noisy humor of a family that revolves around three very different brothers and the women who love them. From Diane's side you get the affectionate hilarity, tenderness, and occasional explosiveness of three sisters and their mom—and a dad who has spent a lifetime just sitting back and grinning wryly at his brood.

Every day is the best of times and the worst of times—sometimes at the same exact time. Our three nieces and two nephews are endlessly amusing, engaging, and exhausting: they want to play poker before breakfast (especially Miranda, a cardsharp since the age of six), run wild on the beach all day, draw or become Game Boy zombies until the ice-cream truck comes, go to the arcade, and then come back and play charades or put on a show until they drop.

At any given moment, someone's laughing, crying, fuming, having a breakthrough conversation, or not speaking to someone. It's a magical, hysterical, and emotionally taxing week, engaging in every way. And when it's over, Diane and I come home so mentally overloaded that we can barely function.

This year we decided that someone needed to invent a new medication that would block memories of all the pressures of intergenerational family life without inhibiting the joy. Diane named the drug "FamilEZE," and before long we were both writing jingles for it.

Not only is hers better than mine, but it's the first pharmaceutical jingle ever to include a side effects warning. It's set to "America the Beautiful."

> *Oh Fam-il-EZE*
> *Spells fast relief*
> *Of stressful mem-o-ries*
> *From recent family gatherings*
> *A whole week at the beach!*

Ask your doc-tor please
For Fam-il-EZE
'Twill bring us all world peace
Reclaim thy brain
Your kin's to blame
(and may cause psy-cho-ses).

FamilEZE is endorsed by the support group "Children of Parents." It is available in pill, liquid, patch, IV, and suppository forms.

Just Say "Yes, Dear"

I like going to weddings because when you hear other people taking their vows, it's a good opportunity to reflect on how well you've been keeping your own. If you look closely at the guests during a wedding ceremony, you can usually tell by their body language how couples are doing. You see everything from spouses, like us, who still hold hands to disgruntled lifers who are fidgeting after each item on the matrimonial checklist: Love? Maybe. Honor? Occasionally. Forsaking all others? Um, let me get back to you on that.

After the ceremony ends and the drinking begins, wedding reception chatter quickly moves from deconstruction of the bridesmaids' dresses to speculation on the chances the newlyweds will actually make it—and

then on to bold pronouncements about marital strategies. At a recent black-tie wedding, a guy came up to me
while I was watching the couple have their first dance.
Holding a drink (not his first) and puffing on a fat cigar,
he turned to me and bellowed, "You wanna know the
key to a successful marriage? I can sum it up in two
words."

And they are?

"Yes, dear!" he said, laughing uproariously as he wandered off, ice tinkling in his glass, to share his wisdom
with others.

Ten minutes later, another well-lubricated guy came
up to me with a variant.

"You know, in my marriage, I always have the last
word," he said. "And the last word is 'yes-dear.' "

Normally I don't pay much attention to backslapping
party advice, but this stayed with me because this phrase
perplexes and fascinates me. According to a study on
"conjugal communications" in the *Journal of Marriage
and the Family,* you'd be hard-pressed to find any two
words with a wider range of possible meanings in a relationship, since they can connote "affection or hostility,
interest or disinterest, encouragement or discourage-
ment."

I believe these are the two most passive-aggressive
words in the entire marital lexicon. I can't imagine why
any woman would want to be married to someone who
constantly "yes, dear"ed her.

What do you want, a bobblehead for a husband?

I think that the women who subscribe to this particular theory of marital bliss don't really understand what's going on when their husbands say "yes, dear." Let me explain. While I'm pleased to announce that I've made some progress on my socks—a higher percentage of which now reach the hamper—I'm still having trouble getting dirty dishes from the sink to the dishwasher. On the nights (or mornings) when Diane doesn't buy my standard excuse—that I'm letting the dishes soak—we get into another of those extremely one-sided "discussions" I so enjoy.

Now, it may seem that the easiest thing for a husband to do in this situation is just say "yes, dear." But it's not that simple. If you say "yes, dear" too early in the harangue, you can actually make matters worse and increase your risk of getting whacked upside the head. (This is especially dangerous when dishes are involved—much safer with socks.)

I try to stay with my wife's lecture for as long as I can, and then my mind begins to wander: What's on TV tonight? Should I get new glasses? Will the Sixers make the playoffs?

At this point, I start feeling bad because I know that I'm about to completely tune her out, which I'm pretty sure violates at least one of my wedding vows. But a husband who really knows his wife well realizes that it still may be too early to play the "yes, dear" card. What we're looking for here are the telltale signs of oxygen deprivation—fewer words in the fourth or fifth repetition of the complaint, a flush in the cheeks, perhaps the need to steady herself with a hand on the kitchen counter. When she obviously needs to stop for a deep breath, this is the perfect moment for a "yes, dear."

Personally, I don't believe in trying to say it sincerely because "yes, dear" is, on its face, insincere. I have, over the years, developed a more ironic "yes, dear" that I deliberately deliver in an obviously nebbishy voice to offer some comic relief to the situation. It lets Diane know that I heard her the first five times. It acknowledges (sort of) that I realize I deserve the tongue-lashing. But it also lets her know that I sincerely don't want to become a bobblehead husband in a "yes, dear" couple. I don't know if she ends up feeling she has been heard, but she does usually giggle (my wife has a really great giggle) and is then able to resume her regular life.

There actually has been some academic study of the phrase "yes, dear." Several years ago, a debate erupted when a leading psychological researcher from the University of Washington challenged one of the main therapeutic techniques used with communication-impaired couples—"active listening," where one partner (okay, it's the husband) is encouraged to repeat what he's being told as proof that he heard it. The psychologist claimed his studies showed that husbands needed to say "yes, dear" *more* often. He had come to believe that the main problem in marital communication isn't that husbands don't listen, but that they actively resisted being influenced by what they hear their wives say, simply as a way of maintaining their "manly" power.

While the psychologist had an interesting point, his "yes, dear" solution was widely derided in the media. This somehow failed to keep his book off the best-seller list, which just shows how much couples want to be told that "yes, dear" is the key to a successful marriage.

Last night, over dinner, Diane and I had a long talk about this (and, if you must know, yes, a casserole dish is still soaking in the sink). We began to discuss how these "yes, dear" scenarios generally play out, and I figured it was a good moment to ask if there was any way for us to improve our "conjugal communications." She thought about it for a second, took a sip of wine, and said, "Well, you could actually do these things without my asking."

Or, I could find someone to make me a life-size bobblehead.

Healthy Difference
of Opinion

I'm a big believer in going to the doctor—as long as my wife is the one who is going. And she feels pretty much the same way about me. So when one of us gets sick, we have a lot of inane discussions like this:

"You should've had a physical," I tell Diane as she sits, wrapped in a comforter, trying to get some soup down to quell the antibiotics churning her stomach.

"I told you, I'm not getting a physical until you see the dentist."

"Well, I'll go to the dentist once you get your physical."

"Why should I get a physical when you still haven't done those smear-test things from your *last* two physicals? You do understand that they won't detect internal bleeding while the samples are sitting in an envelope on your dresser, right?"

And so on.

We've been having some version of this exchange for years. But as couples age together, the same exact conversation can end up being about something completely different. Before, they were just preventive medicine "double dog dares." Now what underlies them isn't so funny. It's the unspoken fear between loved ones that says: "If you die before me—of something that could have been prevented—I will never let you live it down."

I do so miss the days of "it's probably nothing." When I was single, and even after first being married, whenever I didn't feel well I always assumed it was probably nothing. And, if I did worry, there was always someone around to reassure me. Headache? Backache? Probably nothing. Quit your bellyaching. And, by the way, that bellyache? Probably nothing.

But now my wife and I—and all the couples we know—seem to have changed the default setting to "it's probably something." Fungus on my foot? Could be toenail cancer. Itchy scalp? Could be follicular Ebola.

Not long ago, whenever my back would go out, as it has periodically since puberty, I always anticipated a speedy and complete recovery. Now when I have back attacks, I am nearly paralyzed by fear that I will never walk erect—or do anything else erect—again. Actually my back just went out. This happened because...well, who knows why? It's never because I was lifting an anvil or a piano and forgot to bend at the knees. It's always because I slept on it the wrong way or inhaled too emphatically.

In general it's always better if married people get sick one at a time. If you have kids or pets, it's always preferable that one of you is well enough to feed them. And within the couple itself, it's best if both are clear on who is the caregiver and who the caregivee. During illness, defenses are down and hypersensitivity reigns, and it's easy to say mean things you don't necessarily mean. Only one spouse at a time should be able to invoke illness—"sorry, babe, it was the drugs talking"—to get out of such emotional jams.

When both of us are ill, we see all the gender differences in nurturing—and in suffering—up close and personal. Diane will be the first to tell you I have a spectacular bedside manner (when I am actually able to sit by the bed without lightning bolts shooting up my spine). But when my back is all twisted up, I can be cranky, annoying, and needy. I don't think I ever quite reach the stereotype of the whiny babies that men are supposedly reduced to at the slightest hangnail. And I'm sure none of my basketball buddies ever think they do, either—although I wouldn't want to eavesdrop on a conversation among the hoop wives on the subject.

Actually, we've reached the point in our marriage that whenever I act testy, Diane will look at me compassionately and ask, "Your back's sore, isn't it?" (Only an idiot would say, "No, my back is perfectly fine.")

Diane, on the other hand, believes that no matter how sick she is, she must do the laundry and clean the kitchen. I ask her not to, but she seems strangely un-compelled by my suggestion that surely we can survive in our own filth for a few days. Instead she stands there lecturing me—and then, when I go back to the couch, yammering to herself—about the countless chores that women get stuck with no matter the situation. If she were in an iron lung, with both arms in casts, she would still be trying to figure out a way to scootch over to the kitchen sink so she could keep tidying.

Last night she dragged herself, sick with aches and chills, into the darkened bedroom and because she had insisted on doing one more load of whites, tripped over the pile she had sorted out and literally flipped right into the empty basket. If that happened to me, the para-medics would have needed to get the Jaws of Life. But not my wife. She got up, dusted herself off, and pro-ceeded to collapse into bed.

There's a resilience about women, even at their sick-est, that I find inspiring and a little scary. Today, com-pletely out of the blue, Diane decides that the best way to treat my symptoms is to challenge me to an ask-your-doctor discussion about the safety of my painkillers. I try to convince her that this little debate, while lively and fascinating, is probably not the best way to alleviate my back pain and ask if maybe we could discuss epidurals.

She nods as if she understands. But I can see that she is humoring me, and in the game of marital chess she's already three moves ahead.

"Okay, fine," she says, "I'll stop harassing you. But only if you agree to call the doctor tomorrow and schedule a physical."

"All right already, I'll do it."

"I want it in writing." She reaches for her desk calendar and writes the following: "I, Stephen Fried, promise to make an appointment for a complete physical" and draws a line where I can sign. And I do.

Oh, she's a crafty one.

So in two weeks I have a doctor's appointment. I'm hoping to God that my back is no longer sore by then. (In my experience, most serious symptoms abate about an hour before you finally get in to see the doctor about them.) But Diane had better be careful. Because she knows that part of the reason I hate going to the doctor is my fear that it'll awaken my secret medical fantasy. Deep inside, I actually want every diagnostic test known to man. I want everything from my eyelashes to my toe hairs analyzed. I want dye sent through every vein, artery, and capillary in my body, and then I want to be x-rayed and CT-scanned from every conceivable angle. Then it's on to the total-body MRI. And not just once. I want an MRI machine set up at the front door of my house. I want to be scanned every morning when I leave and every evening upon my return.

My computer gets a virus check every day. Why, oh, why can't I?

So you want me to go to the doctor, dear? Like so many things in marriage, be careful what you wish for.

She's Such a Good Sport

They say you should never marry someone expecting them to change. But that's a myth. In fact, you should marry someone assuming they will change. But it will always be in some absurdly unpredictable way—and never the way you wanted them to change.

Here is one big way I've changed: When Diane and I got married, I was one of the only men I knew who didn't give a damn about sports. Didn't read the sports page. Hardly ever watched sports on TV. Went to Super Bowl parties pretty much for the big buffets.

Generally, I was baffled by my friends and their obsessions with sports. Which I guess made me more like a typical wife. And, like too many wives, I learned to fake it. This was especially easy during football season, since teams play only one game a week and it's simple enough to get the gist from the TV news teasers (home team won, be happy) so you can nod knowingly in the locker room.

I always knew Diane really appreciated that I wasn't like the other guys. And I remained that way for so long that she had every reason to believe that my non-interest in sports had reached some sort of tenure status in our marriage.

So imagine her distress when I suddenly began morphing into a raging NBA basketball fan. It began innocently enough. Several years ago, some friends of ours conned us into buying half of their season tickets for the Philadelphia 76ers. I initially saw this not so much as a commitment to sports but as a commitment to twenty nights out. (Just like anything else married people subscribe to, it's more about getting out together than seeing the Belgian touring company of *Les Misérables*.) I even thought Diane might enjoy coming to some games, but she only came when she felt sorry for me because one of my guy-dates bagged out at the last minute. And then she spent most of the time drawing amusing caricatures of players, fans, and cheerleaders in a little sketchbook.

She was missing what turned into a magical year in hoops. Much to everyone's astonishment, the team suddenly got really good. In fact, we—yes, I had started thinking of the 76ers and me as a "we"—made it all the way to the finals against the Shaq/Kobe Lakers, the

NBA's evil empire. And somewhere in the middle of those dizzying playoffs, I became hopelessly addicted.

I started memorizing the sports pages, obsessing over substitution patterns and obscure stats. Around the guys, I could suddenly talk the talk.

At home, however, this made things a little weird. Diane was confounded by these changes. I was turning into a "*guy* guy" and she had gone out of her way to marry someone who wasn't. She did her best to tolerate my aberrant behavior and adjust to having an ESPN-pecked husband. She only really complained when I began insisting that any televised basketball game should automatically edge out whatever program we would usually watch on our only TV, the one with the dysfunctional VCR.

For the better part of two years, the 76ers came between us. And then, during the third season, something even more surprising happened. One night I called from the car, because I was coming home late from an interview. All I heard was a woman's voice saying "you would not *believe* what Allen just did!" At first I thought it was a wrong number, until I heard "but wait, baby, hold on a second...Ah, *c'mon,* man, that's a *foul!*"

It took me a second to get my bearings. I was feeling a little light-headed. Diane was *watching the game?* On purpose? Without me?

When I got home, she recapped the highlights for me just like...well, just like an actual fan. I wasn't sure how to react. I can imagine some husbands being upset by such a turn of events—they *like* the barrier that sports provides between them and their wives, and wouldn't want it toppled any more than they would want to join their wives' book group. But I had a different concern. I was afraid that if I asked what had happened, it might break the spell she was under.

Eventually she explained that her transformation came gradually, through repeated viewings of the super-human exploits of Allen Iverson. The greatest non-tall athlete of all time, he became a source of constant fasci-nation for my five-foot-one wife—who, it turns out, was a pretty good athlete as a kid (until reaching the age when, in her small town, the only sport open to girls was being a cheerleader for the boys' teams). The endless drama surrounding Iverson eventually led her to bond with some of the other players. Whatever rules and strat-egy she didn't remember, she'd ask me about—or go on the Internet. (I love it when she quotes from ESPN.com.)

Today, Diane is a bona fide hoop fan. She comes to most of the games—she knows to skip the crummy teams—and really appreciates the finer points of the sport. (Although, I must admit, I do sometimes miss the cheerleader sketches.) And I'll never forget the first time she leapt into my arms after Allen Iverson made a buzzer-beater to win a game: I swung her back and forth and found myself in a whole new kind of love.

I may have been genetically predisposed to marrying a latent sports fan. Growing up, my mom was actually much more into sports than my dad. Raised outside of Pittsburgh, she always went with her father to see the Pirates and the Steelers. The last year of Grandpa's life, the Pirates were in the World Series, and the final game was on a Sunday when we had tickets for the local community theater. So while my father and I sat watching some guy from Harrisburg warble "Some Enchanted Evening" in his best French-waiter accent, my mother and my brother listened to the game, swapping the earpiece of a black transistor radio. I can still see the tears running down Mom's face when her beloved Pirates won it all.

I've had friends say they envy me that my wife has become a basketball fan. Their wives will barely let them surf over to the game to check the score during the commercials for *Desperate Housewives*. I tell them it's great, but like many things in marriage, more complicated than it looks.

I have known couples where the wife kinda plays along with the husband's sports obsessions so she won't feel left out. You can usually spot these couples because the wife is trying a little too hard, and conveniently has all the same opinions and favorite players as the husband. But Diane has her own take on the sport. For example, we roundly disagreed on whether the team should trade its fading point guard, Eric Snow, and when they did, she became despondent and weepy. When our team started getting eliminated from the playoffs, she began rooting, rather brazenly, for a team I despise—the Detroit Pistons. Now that the Sixers have broken our hearts and traded Iverson, Detroit is her favorite team, period. She has actually adapted their swagger, and sometimes gets so Pistony I worry she will trash-talk me in bed.

So now I'm a guy who gets into sports arguments with his wife. Eventually, I'm sure I'll win one.

The High-Tech Manservant

For as long as I can remember, I have been my wife's technology manservant. While I am utterly useless when it comes to any apparatus used for home repair or chores, I've always been in charge of all the "higher devices"—anything described with the word "mega" or "giga."

It has also been my *fault* if these higher devices don't work, even if the real blame belongs to the manufacturer—or to Diane herself for resorting to "panic pushing." That's when she pushes one button, and when it doesn't do what she thought it would do—or doesn't do it fast enough—she pushes other buttons, and eventually *all* the buttons. And then she's surprised when it turns out she has just ordered her computer to destroy every file she has ever created, and then to blow up her printer. She has wrought similar havoc on her cell phone, our TV, and the microwave (which, with the proper sequence of buttons, can actually be a weapon of mass destruction). Each time, my fault.

So far, she has spared our new digital camera, but only because she's afraid to touch it at all until she has time to study the seventy-five-page manual.

I believe only Stephen Hawking could grasp how much time that would really take.

To make matters worse, I am—like many of my fellow husbands—now servicing not only my wife but a large extended family of impatient "low-tech ladies." Over the past couple of years I got it into my head that it would be a good idea to help my mother, my mother-in-law, and my sister-in-law (along with her two daughters) buy computers, Internet service, digital cameras, and DVD players. I figured that if they all had the same models and service that I did, it might be easier to help if they *occasionally* needed a hand.

I'm now handling so much family tech support that I may have to outsource *myself* to India.

In the middle of all this, Diane decided she wanted to switch from a PC, which is what we've used for twenty years, to a Mac, which she heard was more "user-friendly." Needless to say, we have yet to meet any of these befriended users. And even after taking a college course on how to do Mac graphics, she still prints out every page she creates along the way in fear the machine will eat her work.

There was a time when being the technology manservant was actually kind of charming. I recall somewhat wistfully those early days of marriage—and of high-tech—when Diane would call for me from her home office with a computer problem. I'd come bounding into her room, stand behind her, and reach her keyboard by putting my arms around her—the same way guys used to teach their gals how to golf. Then I'd fix the problem with a keystroke or two, and feel very manly, very modern.

The same was true when I had to help Diane work the other contraptions that laid the groundwork for the techno-chivalry of the '80s and early '90s—first-generation VCRs, cordless phones, answering machines, CD players, Walkmen, digital watches, all those groundbreaking inventions that are now sitting in the basement because it seems criminal to throw away something in which we invested so many dollars and so many hours.

As I kept coming to Diane's tech rescue, I did wonder why an otherwise modern couple took on such traditional gender roles only with these gadgets. I worried this was because of something I was doing—was I deliberately trying to keep my wife barefoot and unable to work the spell-checker? Or, was she, and other wives like her, suffering from some kind of "compu-rella complex," where they actually *preferred* to be repeatedly saved? Either way, I assumed the need for my technological gallantry would be short-lived—that as soon as these machines became more commonly used, cheaper, and easier to run, I would never again find Diane weeping at her monitor, croaking out "the horror, the horror."

Today, I know better. While I certainly know many women who are digital whizzes, they are usually people who have to be for their professions. In most couples, there is still a large tech disparity, and it usually involves the husband being responsible for care and maintenance.

Why is this still true? One friend suggested to me that wives have the same passive-aggressive attitude toward "our" devices as we have toward "their" vacuum cleaners and washing machines. Actually, I think it's a different passive-aggression, because I don't really *want* to know how to work the Dyson, but Diane really *does* want to be able to watch a DVD without my assistance. Granted, I am sometimes embarrassingly impatient with Diane when I can't breezily solve a tech problem for her, and I can be even worse with my mom. I do recognize how this mirrors their impatience with me during a lifetime of failing to perform household tasks to their satisfaction. But there's something more to this, some way that these new technologies push our primal marital buttons.

For advice and solace, I call my friend Tim, who has

been my tech guru since floppy disks were actually floppy. What husbands never want to admit to their wives is that most of us really don't know all that much about these devices, either. We just know more than our wives do. And we all know a guy like Tim, who doesn't mind occasionally serving as *our* technology manservant, allowing us to look smart to our spouses.

We're also not ashamed to call our Tims. So I suspect we ask for advice sooner, and more frequently, than our wives would ever believe. I know Diane feels insulted when I suggest she ask me for advice earlier in the predictable cycle of giga-aggravation, or even call tech support herself. She thinks I'm dissing her. I'm not. I'm just trying to convince her that we all need a Tim (which she finds hard to believe even though she sometimes "Tims" for her mother).

I have always been curious how my Tim, who brought compu-comfort to so many, handled the tech divide in his own marriage. Apparently, no better than me—which I find comforting.

"It's funny you should ask," he said, "I just got off the phone trying to help my wife with her iPod—with only moderate success." Particularly dangerous since iPods are so much easier to throw on the floor and stomp on than computers.

Tim says that while he has been the tech guy at the office for years, he finds ministering to the technology needs of his wife and other family members "a massive responsibility. The worst part is that if something doesn't go exactly right they look at you like you killed their puppy. The flip side of all this trust is this deep sense of disappointment."

I know that look well. And I doubt Diane would ever believe how hard it is to fail as her high-tech manservant. This happens more and more often now that she's on the Mac, a machine that sometimes makes me feel digitally impotent. As much as I enjoy being able to solve her tech problems—which is the closest a guy like me will ever get to, say, being able to fix a car—that's how much I hate failing in front of her.

Sometimes it's hard to be a *tech*-man.

Still, there are some technological joys in marriage. Diane has scanned a lot of her drawings and paintings from over the years, and for my birthday made me a book of the pieces most personal to us and our relationship—a gift only made possible by what she learned in her graphics class. And, sometimes, out of nowhere, I'll receive a flirty little e-mail from her and I'll write a similarly flirty one back—like we're back in high school passing notes to each other in the digital hallway. After a half-dozen exchanges, I'll get one inviting me up to her office—for help with something that requires no devices at all.

Husbandry for Not-So-Dummies

The question came up while we were sitting around after Sunday morning basketball, holding on to those last few moments of sweaty camaraderie before returning to our married lives. One guy's wife and kids had been away, and he was trying to come up with a project to do around the house so it would seem like he hadn't just been screwing around and, say, playing basketball the whole time they were gone. He thought maybe he'd scrape an outside wall of the house and repaint it. But we immediately torpedoed that idea.

"That is *way* too much work," I said. "You don't need to do an actual job. What you're looking for is more of a high-profile gesture. Something small and easy that will attract maximum attention. Maybe polish something— a blender or a toaster or something."

"Yes," another player agreed, "something shiny. They're attracted to things that are shiny."

"How about cleaning out the refrigerator?" someone suggested. "All you have to do is throw almost everything away and it will look clean."

"No, no," the home-alone husband said, sternly. "My wife is in charge of the refrigerator. She knows *everything* that's in there. She'll know what I did."

The conversation digressed into several other plans, each involving tiny amounts of extremely noticeable work. Eventually, we realized that what we were really talking about was something much larger. It was all the things we do to manipulate our wives into thinking we are good husbands—while goofing off as much as possible.

"Y'know, what we need is a *manual*," one sweaty guy said, his voice brightening.

"Yeah, we should write one!"

Husbandry for Not-So-Dummies: How to Goof Off and (Almost) Never Get in Trouble. Sure to be a huge seller.

I can even imagine the cover photo, the quintessential goofing-off image: a pair of men's feet, okay, *my feet,* being elevated ever so slightly so Diane can run the sweeper under them without me actually getting up off the couch and missing anything on the five channels I'm surfing.

I am perfectly suited to write such a manual, because I have to cover for my goofing off more than most husbands. Since Diane and I don't have kids, or even pets, there's never anyone else to blame for our occasional chaos. Also, Diane has unusually rigorous—some might say "obsessive"—ideas about how the house is supposed to be maintained in her absence. When we're about to go away, she insists on adding to the stress of packing by tidying the entire house. (In case something happens to us, she wants to be remembered as having a clean home.) So when she returns from a trip, I know she will rush into my arms and kiss me passionately with one eye closed—while the other surveys the extent of damage done in her absence.

But it's not just the mess she's looking for, it's evidence of the waste. My wife is pretty tolerant of almost anything I want to do—except if I don't want to do anything. There's nothing Diane protects more ferociously than her time. Her goal is to maximize her ability to focus on her writing and her artwork, but the thing I find amazing is how much time she spends bemoaning her lack of time. I saw a study once of dual-career couples and how they spend their downtime: it said the men tended to do whatever they wanted, while the women spent a lot of their downtime trying to organize their *up* time. That sounds like us.

Like most men, I am a complete time slob, a holy goof-off. For example, you have no idea how many games of solitaire I played on the computer while writing this. Or, how often I . . . oh, sorry, I have to check my e-mail again.

As a preview of my manual, here are some of my favorite ways to cover up for goofing off.

1. Start any household job as close to the deadline for completion as possible. This ensures that when your wife gets home, you'll still be doing it, bringing more credit for your effort than you deserve. And there could be an added bonus—if she needs you to help her unpack the car, or wants your undivided attention while recounting everything her parents or siblings said (during the visit, as well as during the lifetime leading up to it), she may absolve you from finishing the job. (This works really well if you get particularly sweaty or are making a bigger mess by doing the job than by not doing it.)

2. When picking this job to do as late as possible, stay away from anything she has actually been nagging you to do. Those tasks should always be done when she is at home, in case it turns out she doesn't like how it looks or changes her mind. (This is especially true with hanging things: never put a nail into an otherwise bare wall without complete and verifiable spousal approval.) If you choose something she would never think of doing, like rearranging the stereo components, you have far less chance of doing it wrong.

3. Be especially careful when picking a job involving the kitchen, the bathroom, or closets. These are the

places where wives concentrate most of their organizational attention, so if you're going to clean out or reorganize something in them, you'd better stick to items that have literally gone untouched for months, or even years. Like the muffin tins, or the LPs.

4. If you are going to actually throw things away—rather than just moving them around, alphabetizing, or color-coding them to make it look like you've contributed—here are some simple rules. Feel free to throw away *anything* you brought into the marriage (that she hasn't already). But never ever, *ever* throw away anything she brought into the marriage. That's probably what she did prematurely with all her favorite stuff (imagine what those embroidered bell-bottoms would fetch on eBay today) and you don't want to re-push that red button. If you're really tempted to throw something away, call her on the cell phone for permission—which has the added benefit of letting her know before she gets home that you're doing something besides watching television. (Make sure you mute the TV before calling, or you are a dummy.)

5. If you want to address a problem pile of dirty clothes without actually doing any work, I have two words for you: "dry cleaner." Whatever it costs, it's worth it to know you can make the entire pile someone else's problem. (Don't forget: no starch on the boxers.)

I offer these tips in the spirit of bettering relations between the sexes. Feel free to discuss these strategies— or any others you can think of—with your husband so that he knows *you* know them. (Nothing blows me away more about married life than when my wife makes a casual reference to something I regarded as a well-kept secret.) I mean, if he's going to goof off, he should at least have to work a little harder at it.

Don't Take My Wife, Please

Diane left some letters on the kitchen counter for me to mail, as she always does, and as I walked down the steps I quickly looked through them, as I always do. Among the endless bills was a hand-addressed envelope to someone whose name I didn't recognize in another state.

I thought for a second about asking Diane who this person was, but I didn't want to appear, y'know, suspicious. So instead I went down to my office and acted suspicious, searching the name and address on the Internet. I finally found it on a government scientific web site. And while I tried not to jump to any conclusions, I couldn't get my mind to stop considering the possibility...

Is my wife cheating on me with an algae researcher?

I wrote down the name and address on a Post-it (easier to eat if I had to destroy the evidence), mailed the mail, and went about my business. For the next two days I thought about how to bring this up to Diane. Then I got an e-mail. It was from the algae researcher. Oh my God. I clicked it open and there was just one sentence:

"Did you get the swizzle sticks yet?"

That mystery letter? A check Diane had written for something I forgot that I'd bought on eBay.

Okay, I'm an idiot. I'm also a jealous guy. Always have been. Probably always will be. If twenty years of marriage to a woman who loves and completes me hasn't cured me, nothing will.

Jealousy is one of the few emotions that husbands have always been expected to express. Unfortunately, most of us express it really badly—often for absolutely no good reason, and sometimes with disastrous consequences. It might be the only emotion that wives wish husbands *would* suppress.

After the swizzle stick episode, I started asking my basketball buddies about jealousy—what Shakespeare called "the green-eyed monster which doth mock the meat it feeds on." (I didn't mention Shakespeare specifically because I didn't want anyone to throw the ball at my head. It was bad enough I was asking them to admit they actually had *feelings*.)

I was most interested to hear from one guy because I know he and his wife just entered a scenario rife with betrayal possibilities. After many years of being home with their kids, his wife took a job at a company with a lot of younger single people. I was at a party recently where I saw her with some of her new male colleagues. They flocked around her, almost flirtatiously, I thought. It actually made me feel a little jealous on my buddy's behalf.

So I was amused by the way my friend denied the role of jealousy in his marriage. "Not as big a deal now as it was twenty years ago," he said, "but I've always had more to be jealous about than my wife, because she is a first-class flirt." Then he added, a bit irritably, "Look, her coworkers are all much younger and/or gay. And the one person she is hanging out with a lot is ten years younger, with a pregnant wife."

Oh, okay. Good thing you're not feeling threatened. And, of course, guys *never* cheat on pregnant wives.

How he stays calm I don't know. I get jealous over much less. I'm not what experts call "morbidly jealous." I don't get aggressive or have much of a temper. But I do feel more jealous than any happily married man should. And it comes out in all kinds of little ways I'm embarrassed to admit. Besides occasionally checking out the mail (or, okay, the cell phone bill), I definitely do the "husbandly hover." I pay a little too much atten-tion to whom Diane talks with at parties, remaining far enough away to be inconspicuous but close enough to stealthily intercede in any conversation that seems suspiciously long.

Why do husbands do this kind of stuff? During our first few years together I believed my actions were well-founded responses to something real—perhaps a carry-over from fighting off other suitors to win Diane's hand. Like many husbands I felt I had married someone way better than I deserved and needed to diligently protect myself against losing her. I still feel that way and still see how Diane attracts people: She's smart and disarmingly funny and still turns heads (sometimes all the way around) in just a T-shirt and jeans.

But I have also come to understand that most of my jealousy is unfounded and unprovoked—something I brought into the marriage, like that ugly brown sleeper sofa.

According to social scientists, husbands and wives are jealous in different ways: supposedly, men care more about sexual fidelity and women care more about emotional fidelity. And I've noticed that one important sociological indicator—bad movie dialogue—does bear this out: it is usually "did you sleep with him?" versus "do you love her?"

But I've always been troubled by this notion that men care more about possessing women than loving them, treating them like toys that nobody else can play with, while women will overlook sexual indiscretions as long as he loves her best. So I'm glad to report that recent studies show jealousy is becoming a more equal-opportunity obsession. Men are now scoring as more emotionally jealous than ever before, and women more sexually jealous. Our worst relationship fears have all begun to even out.

As for us, I consider myself lucky that after two decades together my wife is still kind of flattered by how possessive I can be. Even now Diane recalls as "funny and cute" how, during our courtship, I used to show up "coincidentally" at restaurants where she was dining with friends. ("Funny and cute?" a friend of ours gasped when she later heard about my extreme wooing. "He was a stalker!")

When I recently fessed up to Diane about the algae researcher incident, she found it "hilariously touching." I guess that's because she appreciates the upside of jealousy in a marriage. And no matter how many times she has to deal with me waiting up for her like some '60s sitcom dad on the few nights she goes out with the girls, I can think of only one thing worse for our relationship.

And that would be if I *stopped* being so jealous.

The (Check) Book of Love

I learn more about my marriage while doing our taxes than at any other time of the year. As I wade through folder after folder of statements, bills, and crumpled-up receipts—in search of anything that looks even vaguely deductible—I feel I finally understand our day-to-day lives for the past twelve months.

I see what I spent, what Diane spent without my knowing about it, what the computer and the bank spent automatically without either of us knowing about it (including, for the first time, a mistake this year that was actually in our favor). I see a complete accounting of just how many times we went out to eat, how often we bought from the upscale grocery store (when we could have gotten the same thing for less elsewhere), how much we spent on gifts and on charity. I relive every vacation and business trip through the credit card charges.

People who let software calculate their taxes, or just dump a big bag of receipts on their accountant's desk, have no idea what they're missing.

When I tell Diane about the catharsis I experience at tax time, she gives me a blank stare I recognize as her trying to keep her eyes from rolling. She knows that the only reason I get all excited during my annual journey through the financial flotsam is because she's the one who has to make sense of this stuff every other day of the year. She pays all our bills and files all our invoices. And that was true even before we got married.

Not long after I met Diane in the mid-80s, we went for what I hoped would be a romantic lunch. But when I stopped by the ATM on the way, I discovered there was no money in my account, which I'm sure impressed the hell out of her. So I immediately began babbling that I did, in fact, have money, I just didn't know exactly where it was at that moment.

"Well, okay, then," she said flatly, as she graciously paid for our first date.

Several weeks later, she dropped by my apartment while I was in the midst of preparing my taxes, which back then was not a thrill at all. My kitchen table was overflowing with bills and papers, and my checkbook was splayed open. Diane couldn't help but notice that there were only a few lonely entries in it for the entire year, most of them in some form of hieroglyphics.

Diane's father was a dentist and a Navy man: everyone in her family keeps meticulous records of absolutely everything. She was incredulous that she could be falling in love with someone so fiscally impaired.

It wasn't long before Diane took my checkbook away from me. I haven't seen it since. During tax time, she does briefly allow me to look at her exquisitely legible registry of our checks. But I'm not to touch it. Ever. (I'm not alone in this: studies show that about sixty percent of women balance the family checkbook and pay all the bills.)

In the past few years, my wife has gradually taken over all our investments, too. It all began when she decided she wanted to try playing the stock market. Her maiden choice was a certain chain-store behemoth, because when we were on a road trip in the Southwest in 1995, we saw the company's trucks everywhere we went, even on the most remote rural byways. I thought this was very charming. "Diane's first stock," how adorable. Then, of course, the shares started rising—and splitting. When they were worth ten times what she paid for them, I told her she had just been hired as our investment adviser.

We trust our spouses in many ways, but trusting someone with your money might actually be braver—and riskier—than trusting emotionally or sexually. After all, passion can be reinvigorated. There's counseling, sex toys. But once the nest egg is lost, it's lost. After that, you might not even be able to *afford* counseling. Or food.

I realize that women have been forced to trust their husbands to handle all their money for centuries. Because of our financial role reversal, I now understand what a test of faith it is. The biggest challenge is probably when, as invariably happens, one of our investments bites the dust. When this used to happen on my watch, I was tortured and racked with self-doubt. Since Diane is now making the decisions, it's also now her job to comfort me when we lose money.

I've been talking to some of my friends about how they and their wives handle money. It's not easy, because the only thing couples talk about less in public than their sex lives is the details of their finances. People will go on about how their houses have appreciated or the costs of remodeling. In fact, among my peers, real estate and home improvement have become the new porn. But it's rare to hear married couples talk openly about their money—which probably explains why divorcing couples never shut up about it.

Maybe people are afraid that if they go into detail, financial disparities between couples will become more glaring (and nothing is the same once you know exactly how much more—or less—money your friends make than you). Or, maybe it's just that couples are still processing how profoundly they have changed as financial beings since they were single. When most of our friends married, the women were making as much as or more than the men. And in a lot of cases the couples maintained pretty separate finances for the first few years of marriage. (I recall restaurant outings where we went "double dutch," with our married friends splitting their share.)

But now that we're all well into our forties, the marriages all look more economically traditional. Even in the couples where the wives maintain the more prominent careers, the guys have taken over the majority of the financial matters. And every one of the husbands I know does the household taxes—although I suspect few of them get off on it the way I do.

Diane can't wait for tax time to be over. She gets tired of my snooping into her credit card bills. ("Honey, why aren't there more charges at Victoria's Secret here?") And she wants all her files back intact, before they get sucked into the black hole that is my office. Mostly, however, she wants to make sure the taxes are filed on time, because I really enjoy doing it at the very last minute. In Philadelphia, like many cities, it has become an annual ritual for people—mostly men, I notice—to drive their taxes to the main post office moments before the bell tolls on April 15. Extra post office staff are put on so that we can slow down to 5 mph and toss our returns to a waiting postman without touching the brakes.

The nation's wives scoff at this as government-sponsored procrastination. I just see it as the annual climax to my Joy of Tax.

Playing Through a Foursome

We met a couple at a dinner party about a year ago, and the four of us instantly hit it off. We were similar enough, yet different enough, that there was great potential for that most elusive of adult relationships—a new "couple friendship." That's when two couples become friendly not just because there happens to be a work connection, a kid connection, or a friendship between half of each couple into which their spouses are dragged kicking and screaming. I'm talking about a real emotional rectangle where all four people actually become instant friends.

A year later, I still think we are truly couple-compatible. But there's a roadblock, and I have a pretty good idea what it is.

My wife and I are weird.

Lovably weird, I hope, but still weird, and in a very specific, socially challenged way. In a gender role reversal that may not seem like a big deal but actually is, I am the social director in our marriage. I am the one more motivated to make plans, keep plans, and make follow-up plans. I am, okay, the wife, and Diane is the husband, who can be counted upon when asked to commit to an outing to sigh, "Okay, if we must."

So, in our twenty years together, I've had a lot of discussions that go like this:

Me to another husband: "The four of us ought to get together for dinner sometime soon."

"Okay, I'll have my wife call Diane."

"*Um*, well, maybe you better have your wife call me."

"*Huh?*"

By the way, I'm not trying to suggest that my wife is antisocial. Quite the opposite. Anyone who knows us will tell you Diane is much more charming than I am and infinitely more interesting. Not only is she an ideal guest, but she gives great thank-you note and even greater handwritten acceptance note, treating even the most casual get-together as though we've been invited to the White House. But until we actually leave the house to go see other people, getting her to commit to socializing can be a struggle.

Diane hates tearing herself away from her work— which I find hard to understand since I not only welcome distraction but generally do everything I can to invite it. But, mostly, she resists surrendering all the time required to prepare for nights out. And that I *do* understand. For me, it takes about twenty minutes, from the start of my shower to the last slouching look in the mirror. For her . . . well, let's just say this is the one aspect of socializing where she is still very much the wife.

So you can see the problem. Think of the sheer amount of time and energy all wives need to prepare themselves—shower, hair, makeup, dress, re-dress, ask how she looks, ignore the answer, go re-dress again, and then enter into a round of accessorizing before a period of self-hypnosis to get to her "happy place." If the wife wasn't the driving force in making the plans, what would keep her going through these arduous rituals, once used only to prepare Egyptian queens for burial?

While there are times I wish Diane would take the lead in our social life, I might have a hard time relinquishing the job. It's a position I've held since teenhood, when my house was always the one where people congregated (perhaps because we got cable early, and my mom had developed a technique of refrigerator stocking that allowed her to double the snack capacity of each shelf). If I had my way, the home Diane and I live in (and work in) would be a similar kind of adult clubhouse. But it hasn't worked out that way—which represents, I think, one of the few clear and recognizable compromises I made for love.

Still, I do realize that guys aren't always well suited to

be family social directors. While Diane and I both treasure the integral role our couple friendships play in our
marriage—and in some cases, we rely on them more
than on family—I'm much more openly emotional and
downright competitive when it comes to their care and
feeding. I'm one of those people who treat every friendship with the same intensity that I did when I was a teenager. There's a joke that adulthood is just high school
with money, but it's also high school without free time.
Many of the friend issues you have in high school get
confronted and resolved simply because you see everyone so often. Once you reach the grown-up world of
work and family schedules, it's hard to block out the
time to nurture a full-fledged friendship. Diane can accept this; I don't want to accept this. It's been especially
challenging during the past few years, since most of our
friends have kids and we don't. While I know it's stupid
to feel this way, I sometimes worry I'm losing the competition for our favorite couples' time to a new group
of interlopers, these neighborhood kid-and-carpool
buddies.

When I'm feeling friendship-deprived, I take solace
by looking through our bowling pictures. Early in our
marriage, I decided to find the easiest, cheapest, and
least-stressful way to get our closest couple friends together in one place. So we became the first adults ever
to rent out the kids' party room at a local bowling alley,
where we had pizza and beer and wine served in kiddie

party cups. Then we bowled—pretty badly—and ended the night with a goofy group photo.

That was nearly twenty years ago, and now these annual bowling photos are a slide show chronicling the sagas of our major couple friendships. There are two longtime friends who were on hiatus from my life when the parties began but are now back. While their first marriages didn't click with mine (okay, one wife had me thrown out of the wedding party), they show up pictured with their new spouses, with whom we'll all live happily ever after. But miraculously, our core group has been bowling and talking together once a year since "Love Shack" was blaring on the sound system.

In fact, one year we all got so involved in conversation and catching up with couple friends that, for the first time, we actually forgot to bowl. Several hours later we looked up, saw that our lanes had been given away, and decided we didn't really care. We had spent the time doing something much more important.

Travel Bugs Her

When Diane and I got married, we vowed never to give anniversary gifts—therefore avoiding ever having to memorize that periodic table of marital presentry. (I always forget: in the first year, are you supposed to give rock, paper, or scissors?) Instead, we promised we'd take a trip each year as a gift to each other.

When you first start dating, people always tell you the biggest test of compatibility is going away together. And ever since the first time we went away together (and broke one of the beds at the beach house), we thought such an annual test of compatibility would be a fine thing to incorporate into a good marriage. When you travel, you get the chance to become occasional strangers together; forced out of normal rituals, roles, and routines, almost *anything* can happen.

For example, on last year's trip, Diane had her first run-in with the "shoilet."

We decided to take the train all the way from Chicago to LA. Our first-class cabin on the historic Super Chief was supposed to have a bathroom. In reality, it came with a metal closet about as big as an upended coffin that served as both shower and toilet—or, as we dubbed it, the "shoilet."

Given Diane's claustrophobia and her "stall-o-phobia" (fear of public restrooms), I felt certain this was going to be a nightmare. Instead, every time she went in there, she started laughing uproariously. She also talked to me from in there, which she would *never* do otherwise, expounding on the ingenious features like the sliding plastic window that protected the, um, "shoilet paper."

You think you know somebody...but when you travel with them, sometimes you realize that even after twenty years together, you still have much to learn.

Yet, while we often have such revelatory moments while traveling, Diane is still utterly impossible when I'm trying to plan the next excursion. Getting her to go on a trip is like trying to give a cat a bath. Except, in this case, once the cat finally gets into the bath, she promptly forgets all the screeching and clawing and just starts to purr. And she can't understand why I'm still psychically scratched.

In most couples, one person is the designated travel

planner while the other's job is to endlessly second-guess and complain. I've seen husbands and wives in either role. (One friend admitted, "When I travel with the wife, she makes the arrangements; with the mistress, I make them.") And I'm always happy to commiserate with whoever has the reservations about handling the reservations.

I was talking to a guy friend recently and discovered our mutual dread of planning trips for our spouses. He said on their last trip, his wife criticized every possible destination he suggested, each time asking why they had to go at all, then she vetoed all the flight times he suggested, then the whole time she was packing (three days) she kept asking why they had to go, then she wanted to get to the airport seven hours early, then she criticized his traveling togs ("you're wearing *that*?"), all of which he was, actually, prepared for. What got to him was when she criticized the way he was holding his boarding pass and ID for the security checkpoint.

"Really, Steve," he said, shaking his head, "how many wrong ways can there be to hold a boarding pass?"

When I told Diane this story, she completely sided with the wife—and went on to confirm that there is, indeed, a proper way to hold *anything*, including a boarding pass.

At some point, the unwilling spouse has to finally let go. Diane usually waits until the plane is rolling down the runway. She would probably hold out longer, but

I'm a whiny, white-knuckle flier and I need her support. My fear of flying is not theoretical. The first time I ever traveled with a girlfriend, our plane was hit by lightning and had to make an emergency, slam-down landing—heads between our knees, shoes removed, the whole bit—at a remote air force base. The relationship never survived that flight or that trip. Diane, on the other hand, is immensely comforting through really scary situations. When the plane is bouncing around, she'll rub the inside of my wrist to calm me down.

Once we land, our excursions have a predictable rhythm. Wasted from flying, I turn completely cranky until we've actually succeeded in driving the rental car out of the airport complex and onto the highway. Then I'm fine until we get to the hotel, whereupon we always have one of those little eyefights—you know how couples can argue without saying a word, just through blinking, gaping, scowling, and eye-rolling—because I never want to pay bellmen to carry our bags. To Diane, traveling is all about bellmen. If she could, she'd have them carry *her* to the room on a litter.

As soon as a married couple is alone in a hotel room, there's an essential dynamic at play. With all the usual impediments to having sex suddenly gone, what's your pleasure: tourism or the hotel bed, sunbathing or the double Jacuzzi, fancy restaurant or room service? For at least one spouse—or, if you're lucky, for both—sex (or lack thereof) hovers over many vacation decisions. So just like the relationship-movie conceit where you get the awkward first kiss over with before starting the first date, I say make good use of that hotel bed within the first twenty-four hours at all costs. Then you're both on the same page and, if she hates Coral World, it's just because she hates Coral World.

As the trip progresses, Diane is more able to surrender to the vacation I "forced her to go on" than I am. I'm envious. She has no problem turning off her cell phone and ignoring e-mail, while I get the D.T.'s (digital tremens) if I'm disconnected for too long. She is also more relaxed about money when we travel. At home, she is not a big shopper or splurger—that's generally my job. On vacation, she is more comfortable spending. In fact, she'd order gum from room service if she could. Yet, about halfway through a trip, I start getting uptight about money, and find myself trying to economize in small, inconspicuous ways: undertipping, or scouring the dinner menu for that fine $11 bottle of Bulgarian chardonnay. Often, Diane doesn't even notice. When she does, she'll turn to me and say, "What? You want to start saving money *now?*"

Sometimes the best thing a spouse can do is help you snap back into *un*reality.

Over the years, we've survived a Bermuda Triangle hurricane on a teeny cruise ship, wrong-side-of-the-road driving in foreign countries, a bus tour of a nuclear testing site, and, of course, three days on a train with a shoilet. But it's the tiny moments of travel-induced impetuousness that I treasure most. On the wall of my office hangs a series of four shots of Diane from our first trip to the Grand Canyon. In the gift shop of the historic hotel next to the divine abyss, I saw a toy cowboy holster with six-shooters that reminded me of childhood pictures of Diane dressed in her Bat Masterson outfit. So I got them, and photographed her putting them on and twirling them. Her look of sheer surprise and regressive joy is still infectious.

It is the look I remind myself is possible every time we start planning another trip.

"Uh-huh" Means Never Having to Say You're Sorry

 They say Eskimos have a hundred words for snow. But that's nothing. Husbands have one word that can mean at least a hundred things.

That word is "uh-huh."

It's a simple five-letter word that has led to more marital four-letter words—spoken or unspoken—than any other. Because wives know that if their husbands could, they would probably respond "uh-huh" to every sentence ever spoken to them. And since "uh-huh" can basically be defined as any variant of "yes," "maybe," or "are you talking to *me*?" wives would never know what we really mean.

I'm thinking this could be why the law has always insisted that we come right out and say "I do."

Diane and I recently had a little chat about my

"uh-huh-ing." She is actually quite the connoisseur of "uh-huh," since she is a fiction writer whose best scenes are built on re-creating the sometimes subverbal communications between people. Yet while she has thought more about the term than most, she still hates being ignored—or, worse, getting the "uh-huh" from me that she knows is supposed to convince her she is *not* being ignored.

"Actually," she began, "women say uh-huh *much* more than men do—especially when talking to one another. But to us it always means the same thing—it's our way of encouraging someone to go on, to let them know we're listening. In fact, if a woman uh-huhs her husband, it's because she *is* listening, and probably also cleaning or taking care of kids or otherwise multitasking.

"Men who uh-huh aren't trying to multitask—their goal in life is to *mono*task. If you ever see a woman sitting perfectly still saying uh-huh, call the doctor. Something's wrong—seriously wrong. She may be having a stroke."

I nodded, knowing better than to say anything, lest it be misconstrued (or worse, *accurately* construed).

Instead, I decided to delve into the scientific literature on the word "uh-huh." It turns out that Diane is right: studies routinely show women use the term about three times as often as men. And they all use it as a way of saying "I'm listening, I'm interested, please tell me more."

The men in the studies, however, used the term to, as researchers put it, "express uncertainty"—never fully combining the "uh" and the "huh?" into one exclamation. But I'd say "uncertainty" is just the tip of the ambivalence iceberg. Here are some of the things I have meant over the years when saying uh-huh to Diane.

1. Yes
2. No
3. Maybe
4. Maybe not
5. I acknowledge what you're saying but don't agree with it.
6. I agree with what you're saying but don't feel like acknowledging it.
7. I see your point.
8. I don't see your point.
9. I kind of see your point but don't see the point of making it just at this moment.
10. I wasn't listening to anything you just said and would feel stupid asking you to say it again.
11. I really *want* to listen, but I'm groggy from exertion.
12. I really want to listen—but to *The Sopranos,* so could we continue this conversation when the show's over, if I'm still awake?
13. I wonder if there's any of that pie left?

Luckily, while Diane knows intellectually how many different things I could mean, she is still willing to put up with my uh-huh-ing, to a point. As long as my uh-huh-ing is not egregious, and I occasionally look over and make some eye contact, she will continue talking as if we are actually having a conversation. But then I'll go one uh-huh too far. And suddenly a tornado of emotion will touch down.

"Don't you *uh-huh* me!"

And even though this would be the perfect time to duck into the bathroom, I've learned to remain perfectly still in the hope of staving off the inevitable.

Oh please, dear God, no—not *the pop quiz!*

If I'm lucky—and I haven't been inching the TV volume up too much during the "conversation"—I might know the basic subject I've been uh-huh-ing through and be able to eke out a passing grade in the pop quiz. If I'm unlucky, well, it could be a long night.

I spoke to some of my basketball buddies about their uh-huh strategies. One described a rather elaborate formula for the use of the term, which he has been adjusting over the years. He sees saying uh-huh as the highest form of "passive listening" (a phrase used primarily by management consultants and spouses who are comforted by euphemisms for being a jerk). Personally, I think it's the absolute lowest form of "active listening." But either way it's not the kind of thing we should be encouraging here at the Stephen Fried School of Husbandry.

Anyway, my basketball buddy says in any marriage, the goal is to start with at least a fifty-fifty ratio of passive to active listening in all spousal conversations. He tells me the eventual goal is getting to a ratio of twenty percent listening and eighty percent pretending—while at the same time making the wife believe that the ratio is eighty-twenty the other way. This is done, he says, by strategically sprinkling various response-like phrases among the uh-huhs. There are "no kidding" and "that's amazing." There's also what we used to call in speech class "repetition for effect"—simply repeating the last thing she said followed by a noncommittal commentary: "So you say she liked the blue corn chips better? *Hmmm.*"

Or, he counsels, you can move into more overt PDAs— passive displays of *attention*—like the pseudo questions "really?" and "you don't say?" And if you can ask an in-context question, one that actually follows up on details of the "conversation" . . . well, luck be a lady tonight.

The irony of all uh-huh abuse that goes on in marriages is that the word can actually have positive uses around the house. I have, for example, used it to mean yes, emphatically yes: uh-HUH! I have also used it to show unfeigned fascination with something my wife is telling me: uh-huuuuh.

And Diane recently admitted to me that there's a

slight deviation of uh-huh that, if used properly, can actually have aphrodisiac qualities. "I think just adding an 'm' to it makes it very sexy," she said. "Do it a few times in a row during a conversation, and see how the mood changes."

Umm-hmmm.

Stuck in the Midlife
with Me

A lot of my friends have been talking about midlife recently, which is a bad sign. I was brought up to believe that midlife crises were caused by major life-changing events that made you question *everything*. I now suspect they are, in fact, caused by talking about midlife and thinking about midlife and worrying about "turning points" that will trigger the crisis (is that it, is *that* it?) until you basically *cause* the life-changing events yourself.

I'm waiting in line at the video store, wondering whether the films I've chosen could be the turning point. When I get to the front of the line, I ask the woman behind the counter, who is about my age, what movies men rent when they're having a midlife crisis.

"Horror movies about zombies eating people's heads

off," she says, without missing a beat. "At least, that's what my husband has been watching since his midlife thing started about, well, about ten years ago." He also tends to choose his non-horror movies less by plot or theme than by which Hollywood starlets display nudity, cleavage, or sideage; he's currently making a cinematic study of films in which you can see Helen Hunt's nipples.

My heart goes out to wives trying to make sense of the stuff men do when they approach midlife—a period that, like a lot of things middle in America (the middle class, the midsection), is getting larger and larger. For husbands, it now starts in our thirties, as we ponder the approach of forty, and lasts pretty much as long as we can drag it out. As fifty looms, I'm just getting the hang of it.

In my basketball game, every player is at least at orange alert for midlife crisis risk. Since I'm "the commissioner" of this group, responsible for making sure we have enough players for three games a week, I know immediately when something is amiss. Whenever a guy starts to skip more games, offer lamer excuses, or foul more flagrantly than usual, I know some big midlife pronouncement is only days away.

In the past year alone, six of our regular guys made major life changes, primarily to stay one chess move ahead of a possible crisis. Another chose instead to more fully embrace his midlife madness, and bought an even *bigger* boat. I could have predicted every one of these actions, based on our basketball games. These guys' wives should hire me as a crisis-management consultant. Or, I should start putting money down on it—maybe a midlife-crisis betting parlor (where you could get Vegas odds on individuals) or a mutual fund of products guys seek during crisis.

I shouldn't joke. Midlife is *not* like a box of chocolates. It's not that husbands experience anything physically worse than our wives do—in fact, quite the opposite. It may be the lack of a true menopause that gives men...well, so much *pause,* leading us to spend more time reevaluating our lives than actually living them.

From the time I was a boy, I heard stories of men and their meltdowns: the sports cars, the affairs, the bad facial hair, the medallions. I was taught that I should do everything in my power to avoid becoming that kind of husband. I never saw my father indulge in any of these stereotypical behaviors—although he did become markedly less patient in his forties. So I was a little freaked out when, just after I turned forty, Diane said the most chilling thing to me. I was being short with her—apparently not for the first time—and she looked up at me and said, "Y'know, your father started getting a wee bit testy, too."

I don't have a roving eye or a sudden desire to buy

expensive toys or grow sideburns but, clearly, I'm wrestling with some of the impulses all men have after reaching "that age." I just happen to be winning the wrestling match. So far. (Although nobody has been able to tell me authoritatively how many rounds this goes.)

While men always deny they are having a crisis themselves, they do have elaborate theories about why it's happening to everybody else. One of my friends insists all male midlife pressures are about work, even though they ultimately get played out at home. He sees how guys—you know, those *other* guys—start obsessing about their career disappointments or, sometimes just as bad, get bored because they reached the top sooner than expected and don't know what the hell to do with themselves. So after decades of never thinking enough, they now find themselves thinking *too much*. And instead of setting some new goals, they wallow in why fulfilling their original goals was so, well, *unfulfilling*.

Another friend blames midlife woes on the dilemma of the "new dad." He says that his generation of fathers is more involved in their children's lives than any before, "so the thing I've seen over and over is men looking hard at their lives after the kids are gone. I guess they see a house with just them and their wives, and ask 'is that all there is *for the next twenty-five years?*'"

Only one guy I know was actually willing to admit to

having a crisis. And there was nothing funny about it. In fact, what he said struck me as some of the truest stuff I've ever heard a man confide. While he had always suffered from some mild depression, in his late thirties he was slammed with a combo platter of middle-aging issues and psychiatric symptoms. For nearly two years, he drank too much and, he admitted to me, "for the first and only time in my wonderful marriage, the devil was tapping me on the shoulder." Through the support of his loving and saintly patient wife—who was camped on his *other* shoulder begging him to get medication and supportive psychotherapy—he "stabilized before I did anything too crazy."

Someday, perhaps medical science will develop a pill for all these half-life headaches—Mid-Ecstasy—or some kind of vaccine. In the meantime, we can only monitor symptoms. If you want to look for early indicators—and maybe head some symptoms off at the pass—here's a handy checklist of questions I boiled down from the ones researchers use when studying midlife issues. In the past year:

1. Has your husband had a major change in the workplace (really good or really bad, doesn't really matter)?

2. Has your husband learned anything about you that he never knew, something that significantly changed

the way he saw you, or saw himself? (Again, the thing he learned can be good or bad.)

3. Has your husband learned anything about someone else close to him, or about *himself,* that similarly rocked his world?

4. Has your husband recently fulfilled any life dreams— or learned that, once and for all, a life's dream had been permanently dashed?

Yes, it's a little more existential than your typical magazine quiz. But better (and cheaper) to have these discussions now than outside the lawyer's office, right?

As for me, I think I've been protected so far by two things. I've been self-employed for many years: once you work for yourself, every day can be a mini-midlife crisis that works itself out by lunchtime, and you're only as good as your last (or next) book or article, so all of this is familiar. But, more important, I just happen to really love my wife and rarely blame her for any of the inevitable pressures that come even in a good marriage. Diane has actually accused me of being overly forgiving ("I was *such* a bitch today, I'm sorry." "No, you weren't." "Yes, I *was!*").

In fact, she recently asked if I would consider having a *partial* midlife crisis—just so I would improve my wardrobe and get a better car.

I told her I'd think about it.

Afterstuff

All of these essays originally appeared, in slightly different form, in *Ladies' Home Journal.* My thanks to editor-in-chief Diane Salvatore for inviting me to create the first-ever monthly column about husbandry, and for always playing a hands-on role in its care and feeding. This book would never have happened without her, and her readers, all of whom have been great to me.

Special thanks to my day-to-day editor at *LHJ,* Robbie Caploe, a fine editor and a good soul who expertly negotiated the needs of "her" Diane and mine. Also thanks to the art folks (especially the ones who made that bobblehead of me).

Thanks to all the other magazine editors over the years who helped me learn how to write pieces about men and relationships that would push buttons with both sexes—especially my editors at *Glamour,* Cindi Leive and Jill Herzig, and before them Ruth Whitney and Lisa Bain.

Thanks to my fine research assistants (all undergrads from my alma mater, Penn): Jessica Lussenhop, Dan Kaplan, Jennifer Machiaverna, Jessica Fuerst, Maria Popova, and Jason Schwartz.

Bantam Books has been my home for over a decade, but there's something especially delightful about this project—since the idea was nurtured by people inside the house who read (and occasionally contributed to) my column. Thanks to the book's earliest fan and fairy godmother, my friend Barb Burg. Thanks to publisher Irwyn Applebaum, deputy publisher Nita Taublib, and everyone at the house for their continued support.

My longtime editor, advocate, and mentor at Bantam is the inimitable Ann Harris, whose range, focus, and gusto never cease to amaze. Her willingness to take on this little book in the midst of a big one we've been doing proves to me, again, just how intellectually ambidextrous and warmly encouraging she can be.

Perpetual thanks to my literary agent, Loretta Fidel, who has been guiding me, indulging me, protecting me, and occasionally bitch-slapping me for nearly twenty years now.

I'd like to thank by name all the family members, friends, basketball buddies, and other assorted husbands who have informed these essays directly, indirectly, or, occasionally, against their wills. But I promised I wouldn't. So to everyone who shared with me—and everyone who was surprised, pleasantly or un, to see a personal anecdote in print—my thanks, or my apologies, or in some cases both.

And thanks to my wife, Diane Ayres, for saving (or in many cases writing) all the best lines, and for having the kind of heart and mind that inspire great husbandry.

ABOUT THE AUTHOR

STEPHEN FRIED is an award-winning investigative journalist and personal essayist. He is the author of the widely praised books *Thing of Beauty: The Tragedy of Supermodel Gia* (which inspired the Emmy-winning HBO film *Gia*); *Bitter Pills: Inside the Hazardous World of Legal Drugs;* and *The New Rabbi.* A two-time winner of the National Magazine Award, the highest honor in magazine journalism, Fried has written frequently for *Vanity Fair, Glamour, The Washington Post Magazine, GQ, Rolling Stone,* and *Philadelphia* magazine. For the past four years, he has also written a monthly column on men, marriage, and "husbandry" for *Ladies' Home Journal.* An adjunct professor at Columbia University Graduate School of Journalism, Fried lives in Philadelphia with his wife, author Diane Ayres.

www.stephenfried.com